PICKING YOUR SHOTS

Picking Your Shots

And other stories of dogs and birds and guns and days afield

Steve Smith

Stackpole Books

Published by
STACKPOLE BOOKS
Cameron and Kelker Streets
P.O. Box 1831
Harrisburg, PA 17105

The following stories have been published in magazines:

"Back of Beyond"	*The Drummer*
"The Crazies"	
"The Gun Cabinet Shuffle"	
"The Meeting"	
"The Parson and the Crabapple Dog"	
"The Streak"	
"The Quail Caper"	*Gun Dog*
"Duck Hunters"	*Wildfowl*

Illustrations by Mike Watson

Printed in the U.S.A.

Library of Congress Cataloging-in-Publication Data

Smith, Steve.
    Picking your shots and other stories of dogs and birds and guns and days afield.

    1. Hunting. 2. Hunting dogs. I. Title.
SK33.S643   1986   799.2   86-5789
ISBN 0-8117-1241-9

For Jess and Parker,
and the pooches in my life—
how we hate to see October go. . . . .

Contents

Foreword

There are three types of forewords. The most common ignores the book the foreword writer's supposed to be pushing and pushes the foreword writer's own book instead.

Another flatters the author's work beyond all credibility and thus costs him sales.

The third and most rare is the honest kind—where the foreword writer(me) says that the author(Smith) needs the money and has no other skill to provide for his bird dog or family.

But Steve Smith is not asking for charity—or asking me to ask for him. He is quite able to offer you the rarity of a good laugh as well as the sensitivity to make you say, "That's what it's all about. . ." Steve puts it just the way you always wanted it said and when you think about it, that's why you want a book in the first place.

I've known Steve for years, both personally and through

his writings. He's the sort of friend—and writer—that we have too few of.

This book is mostly funny, which is what most of us need even more than easy straightaway shots and which is harder to come by. Its serious moments are the nice kind, like when your dog puts his head on your knee.

I'd like to ask a favor: After you've read this book two or three times—give it to a youngster to read. You'll be planting the right kind of seed in the right kind of place.

Gene Hill

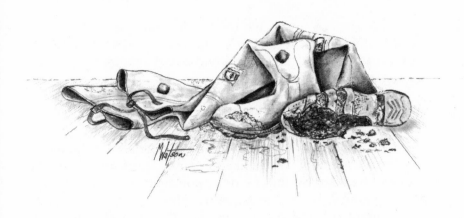

Picking Your Shots

For most of us these days, not taking quite the number of birds the law allows is a common thing; for some of us, it's been a way of life. Spending your days afield and coming up short at the end may, to some, seem like we should be ranked with life's other under-achievers, but I don't guess I agree with that, and not totally out of self defense.

I think that once we've made up our minds that unless the woods are full of patently unlucky woodcock, or we see enough quail to shoot a case of shells at, or unless the ducks darken the sun, we probably won't have to quit early, we have more fun.

When I was in college, I had one of those roommates who attracted girls. When we went to a party together (I always had to come in five minutes behind him so nobody would know we were together), he was always the center of attention. He may have been witty and intelligent, but he made up for it by being handsome.

Anyhow, if we went some place where he, for some bizarre reason, didn't get the adulation he thought was rightfully his, he was sick for weeks.

For those of us who are used to getting life's limits, measured in numbers of things like birds and guns and dogs and cars and bank accounts, the disappointments when we don't can be painful; but for those of us who started off slow and then sort of tapered off, not getting the limit of really anything permits a more genteel, more relaxed way of life.

Living under the limit lets us do some things that others don't do because they don't have time. We can take time to tap the trunk of a hollow tree to see if the flying squirrels are home or eat a big lunch and fall asleep under a yellow sugar maple.

We can take time to teach a small boy where it is that the muskrat goes when he dives under the surface of the brook and we can collect and use fine, classic old guns not because they'll make us better shots, but because we'll feel more like sports while we're missing.

Going through life with my dims on is what some pals of mine accuse me of doing. Maybe that's because those of us who live down under the limit try to take solace in small victories because the big ones are out of our grasp. Victories like a dog that will hold a point, at least for a little while, or being able to make just the right stew at camp, or being able to split wood enough to last the winter without hurting something vital and, at least for now, useful.

Small victories like seeing the first spring robin or hearing the first wedges of Canadas go over in late September or hearing the woodcock do their strange and primitive sky-dance when the spring nights are just right.

Once you've made up your mind, or fate has, that you're likely to live most of your days afield with such victories and without bulging gamebags, you come to appreciate these things; you come to see the outdoors as a total experience, where remembering your thermos is as much a victory as calling in geese, and where on the odd occasion that you remember to tell your Lab to shake outside the blind and not in, and she does, there's actually somebody there to see it and think you two have this shaking thing all worked out.

Let's face it, most of us don't, thank God, have to live by what we shoot. For most of us, hunting is recreation, or at least it's supposed to be. It's the way we have fun. If your fun means that you have to have whatever is the legal limit, fine, I guess. But if you don't feel you really have to, you can be content with what you get, even if what you get is the memory of a grouse that dodged behind a tree, or a spring mushroom, or a kid with his first rooster pheasant.

Not that I won't keep trying to get a little better. I can sit with you at your house and drink your Glenlivet and discuss drop at heel and comb and cast-off and chokes and how square-load 16's in 8 shot are far superior to stringing 20's for going-away woodcock. I've got a bunch of stuff at my place like fine duck calls and compasses and snowshoes, none of which I know how to use very well, and some I'll never get the chance to try.

But, you see, having those things and being able to discuss them and argue about them is what's part of the fun. It doesn't matter to either you or me that the woodcock, if centered, couldn't care less if the load came from a 16 or a 20 — the fact is that three times in four we'll miss anyhow.

For those of us who spend nine months a year yearning for the three months of autumn, no cost is too great. You'll go two out of three with the Storm and Strife over a fifty-dollar lamp, but you'll drop a thousand on an unproven pup without batting the well-known eyelash. Memberships in gun clubs and wildlife organizations and subscriptions to sporting magazines and week-long hunting trips here and there all conspire to make our collective bank balance look not a little like we're on the verge of Chapter 11, but we don't even think of it. If the oldest daughter needs braces, we compute the cost not in dollars to be earned, but in dollars that we can't spend the way *we* want to. (By the way, for the cost of braces, you could get a pretty fair B-Grade Parker with some nice engraving—see what I mean?)

Once, in my youth, I made a bet with another shooter that I could bag more woodcock than he could with a pre-determined number of shells, I guess it was five. We hunted behind his dog, and I won because I didn't shoot at every bird that went up, and he did. He was quickly out of shells and I hadn't even fired and he was mad as hell because he said I was cheating and I was, sort of.

But, like many of the things we learn in life, this little incident taught me more than that woodcock are too fine a bird to be the basis for a bet. It taught me just how enjoyable a day can be when we can consciously control the circumstances. Especially the circumstances surrounding our shooting, which normally ranges from sub-par to rotten. Get a tough flush? Don't shoot; the next one will be easier.

Educators say that when we take one instance and apply it in broad terms to something else, that's called "divergent thinking." Right after I fleeced my companion, I started to let my thinking diverge toward hunting and shooting, and picking my shots.

Picking your shots can be choosing to sit down by a stream in the fall and watch the brook trout fin out their redds on the stream bottom. Or it can be something like eating your lunch at nine in the morning in the goose blind, if that's what you feel like doing. Picking your shots means, simply, having things the way you want them because that's the way you want them.

I like to mosey through the woods when I'm hunting. I like to look at the little red British Soldier lichen that grows in my part of the world. I like to see where the beavers have worked along an alder and aspen run where the woodcock live in two's and three's, and I like the closeup smell of fallen leaves when I stretch out to doze in the litter of a yellow sugar maple. I like to look at my boy's face when he walks in on point; his big green eyes have the white showing all the way around. I like to remember when shooting a lot of birds seemed somehow so important, and I like to wonder why it stopped being so.

A couple of years ago, I was hunting a birch-covered hillside alone in the morning. The night before, a huge wind had blown from the north and the cover was loaded with woodcock. The birds were tired and only fluttered up ahead of my dog. I shot the first one, then unloaded my gun and turned the day over to dog training. It seemed too easy, on the one hand, but on the other, how often can you get woodcock to cooperate and let you handle a pup? I remember that day clearly, much more, I'm sure, than I would if I'd shot my limit.

Once, my dog and I wandered upon a little cemetery in the woods. The graves were marked with rotting white pine slabs, but the carved words could still be read, and I passed an hour reading the history of a forgotten little town. I remember seeing the markers for several children, and I guessed a flu or measels epidemic. I visited with them a little while before I went my way and I told them how lucky they were to have such a nice place to sleep before I told them good-bye.

The older I get, the more a hunt means an opportunity to see something I haven't seen before or see something familiar in a little different way.

For years, I spent every cent I could get my hands on trying to find a shotgun that would make me the slicker I knew I was deep down inside. Finally, not too long ago, I made the decision that the gun I was using and liked the most would be the one I'd probably finish out my days with. I like it because it seems as easy-going and reliable as a good friend. It'll do what I ask it to and very efficiently, but it also enjoys being leaned against a tree so it can watch me soak my feet in a cool stream early in the season. It shoots where I look, and I like that, but I'd probably carry it even if I did nothing but miss with it. Like so much of what we do, it just seems right.

I used to be guilty of keeping track of birds shot in ratio to shots fired, and for a few years I got all tangled up with the long division and percentages and things that go bump in the night. There's nothing wrong with doing this if you're trying a new gun, and most of us are most of the time, but with me the mathematics started to interfere with the hunting. If I happened to be in the right spot and encountered three consecutive star-crossed birds, I started to tighten up and even thought about going home before I hit an unlucky streak. I don't do that anymore.

Instead, I like to take things as they come and chalk up the good days as my dues for all the bad days I've had and know at the end of a season or a lifetime, things ought to come out about even.

Now I leave the math at home and take binoculars with me. When I'm waterfowling they help me pass the time between flights. They're great for looking at shorebirds, settling bets on what kind of ducks those were that passed by without giving us a second look, and what the fellows in the next blind are having for lunch.

The outdoors does something to you and me, it makes us better able to cope with the civilized world, with its unordered ways and ego-breaking tensions. It makes us self-sufficient. It makes us whole.

The Kid

L iving at my house, there's an absolutely superb boy, everything a dad could ask for. A sure-handed short-stop who can throw you out at first from his knees in the hole, a guard on the junior-high basketball team who regularly plunks in 20-footers to draw the opposition out and away from his taller buddies inside, and a kid who has taken naturally to the sporting life which is how I make what passes for a living.

Now if I sound too much like a chest-beating father, let me tell you that this lad has a habit which really bothers me: He almost never misses with a shotgun. That trait alone has caused friendships to end and shooting partnerships to dissolve. But when one of the partners is your flesh and bone, you can't very well leave him home.

The worst part about it is, he never brags on his shooting. I don't mind a guy who brags a little—hell, I do myself on a good day. The reason I don't mind boasting is because it shows me that the braggart has really impressed himself, and he has to let the world know that good days with a shotgun are few and far between, and he's going to get the best possible mileage out of one when it comes along.

But the shooter who takes a tough screamer through the alder tops with a snappy right barrel—and then repeats it a couple of times—and doesn't even mention his skill bothers me. To him, a bird in the air represents a dead bird; there has to be a loud noise before that happens, but it will. That's my kid.

I trained him in the ways of grouse and woodcock. When he was three, I cured him of wanting anything but side-by-side doubles by putting him in a barrel with a picture of an over/under and rolling him down a hill. He started shooting skeet when he was nine, and we worked at getting him just the right gun (with two stocks—one for now, one for when he gets his growth), and finally when he was 12 and could hunt, he was ready. Naturally, I expected his nerves to be the great leveling factor when the birds started coming up under his feet, so I coached him on how to approach the dog when she locked up, how woodcock head for daylight, grouse for cover. Just as naturally, I didn't expect him to remember any of it. But any kid who can steal a basketball and sink a shot from the top of the key at the buzzer has to have inherited his mother's nervous system, not mine.

His first season, he shot something like 60% on wood-cock—that's three birds with five shells, only he shot a lot more than three birds. I wanted him to get some shooting, so I spent a lot of time working the dog and him; I should have worried about my own shooting.

Pheasant hunting was no different—except he missed less. And ducks? I took him duck hunting with Charlie Lichon. Charlie asked The Kid if he'd like to use a spare 20-gauge autoloader with a short stock that was kicking around his basement, and The Kid allowed as how that would be nice. The first flight of ducks decoyed in and The Kid stood and calmly pulled a pair of greenheads from a flock of eight and then "wowed" at how well Charlie's Lab, Jill, went and got them.

So, Gentle Friend, what would you do if you had a kid like this, a kid who wins the four-man pool on a woodcock hunt for fewest shells for a limit taken? You'd figure out a way to put him in his place, right?

Well, you would if you were me. I started making him pop the brush for me, pushing the birds out so I could shoot. They cut his way instead of coming out.

I started making him push fencerows and gullies for pheasants, while I waited at the end to shoot the birds as they flushed to me. Only they didn't—they came curling back over his head and died.

I started making him clean all the birds by himself, figuring that if he shot too well this would discourage him. What I got was, "Gee, Dad, I cleaned my five and your one, and I can't see any marks in yours—I'll bet you scared it and it ran into a tree."

Nothing worked, so I fixed him, I pulled out all the cadmium rods in his little reactor and gave him the ultimate challenge, something to set his teeth on edge, mess up his autumn days, and take forever the gleam from his bright, green eyes. I gave him a pup to train.

Not just any pup, I gave him a male setter, a big—75 pounds—male setter. I didn't know the dog was going to get that big, I just hoped. The dog's name is Parker, and when he stands up, a year-and-a-half old, and puts his paws on The Kid's shoulder, he's taller than The Kid.

I taught The Kid about check cords and whistles, and whoa, and quartering, and hand signals.

And then Parker taught the kid about frustration, and ulcers, and swear words with lots of hyphens. Now, autumn days afield are different. I chuckle while The Kid screams and blows his whistle and his freckles stand out like they do just before one of his karate tournaments. Now, the kid misses and blames the dog. When he hits, it's an accident he doesn't even get to see because he's watching the dog to make sure the mutt stays in the same county. And when *my* female setter's romantic period comes on, The Kid is the one who has to get up to quiet his moaning beast.

Now, The Kid knows the shooting life for what it is—a series of frustrations interrupted once in awhile by a nice day. He now has setter hair all over *his* room and on *his* clothes. Now, best of all, I shoot more birds and he misses—a lot.

Son, welcome to the uplands.

Grouse Camp

Grouse Camp. Once a year. Long weekend. Wisconsin. Be there.

Grouse Camp happens, sort of. It isn't really planned. Well, maybe a little. We've very careful to evaluate weather conditions and woodcock flights to choose the right weekend. But we don't plan things like food or what we'll do if it rains, and it always does. I mean always.

The supporting cast of characters changes from year to year; the core group stays the same. There's Tom Petrie and his brother Charlie. By trade, they are magazine editors and publishers. Charlie is a top-notch camp cook who once spent his professional life as a game warden. His Lab, Baxter, is always with him at Grouse Camp. Baxter looks like a cape buffalo; he is probably the dumbest dog the folks at Grouse

Camp have ever seen. Baxter does stuff like walk into the campfire and stand there until somebody realizes he's on fire and calls him out. One year, Baxter ate a pound of aged brick cheese that was on a table near the fire. Baxter had some problems for four days afterwards and the folks at Grouse Camp were happy about Baxter's problems. At home, when Charlie gets into his cups, he goes out to Baxter's kennel and sits down next to the beast and sings French trappers' songs until his kids drag him inside. Charlie complains that nobody ever says anything nice about Baxter. There are lots of reasons why. Charlie is philosophical about Baxter. The dog hunts and flushes birds and retrieves them for Charlie. But he makes life miserable for everybody while he's making life nice for Charlie.

Tom Petrie has a habit of getting lost all the time. Tom gets lost going to the outhouse. Tom wears two compasses and carries another one in his boot, but it doesn't make any difference. His dog, Sadie, once took off on us for an hour and I finally tackled her by diving over a brushpile while she was rolling in a dead possum. I collared the dog and started hollering for Tom. Tom didn't answer. Tom was lost.

Dave Duffey shows up once in awhile. He always brings a trailerful of untrained dogs he's working, and he insists on driving the trailer around to all our coverts. Duffey always gets the trailer stuck in the biggest mudhole north of the 45th parallel, and then we have to pile out and push.

Duffey always goes at it with Galen Winter, another regular. Galen is a writer and lawyer who shoots, like most lawyers, a bit crooked and to the left of center. Galen and Duffey trade jokes back and forth all night around the campfire, trying to see who can tell the last joke. The rest of us usually take our aching ribcages to bed about three A.M., and sometimes those two are still at it at dawn when we roll out to hunt.

Galen has a recipe for woodcock. He says you should fry the birds in onions and bacon for three minutes, and then marinate them for 24 hours in a mixture of soy sauce, stewed tomatoes, and kerosene. The kerosene kills the taste. Galen has about five recipes for woodcock, all of which feature kerosene somewhere. Every year, somebody comes to camp with a concoction that will make Galen like woodcock. So far, nothing.

The funny thing about Grouse Camp is that we don't get on each other's nerves. The wood gets cut, the cooking gets done, the dishes get washed, and somehow it all sort of happens. Everyone pitches in and helps, and if one of us has had a long drive to get there and is especially tired, the rest of us allow him to sleep a little longer.

Sure, there's the normal joshing about misses—like the time Charlie missed a going-away woodcock flying down a forest road with both barrels, or the time Galen, on three consecutive birds, couldn't find the safety, then couldn't find the front trigger, and when he finally did shoot, none of it mattered because the gun wasn't loaded.

Once a year. Grouse Camp. Be there, friends.

A Primer For Puppies

Okay, so you're a grouse dog puppy who's been brought home by some poor, unsuspecting slob who thinks you're going to make a great dog, one with whom he can share the uplands for years to come, one who will do his bidding and be joyous about each pristine day afield. Well, you've got to set this character (the Big Guy) straight right off or else your life will be nothing but day after day of involuntary servitude.

You see, if you don't establish the upper hand early, things are going to go from bad to worse to ridiculous. We can't have that. Never forget that your bloodlines are better than Big Guy's who, no doubt, resulted from his mother's gate being left open one night lo these many years ago.

So, for starters, let's take a look at what to do to make

sure your life is one of ease and contentment. When you are brought home, make sure that you quickly ingratiate yourself to the Big Guy's mate and his human pups. This way, he will never be able to discipline you in front of them. They'll rush to your defense immediately, which means, over the course of your lifetime, that you can get away with pure, blue, triple-distilled hell whenever they are around. They will be your barristers defending your every delinquent action.

Quickly establish that you get carsick easily. This will stand you in good stead when it comes time to go to the vet where you'll be held down and stabbed with needles. Getting carsick won't stop BG from taking you there, but at least it'll spread the suffering around a little.

When he tosses you in the car—once he's separated you from the furniture you've been holding onto—start thinking about eating live salamanders or something. If you're in the back seat, make sure that you bring up everything you've had to eat for the last 48 hours right onto the upholstery. If you're riding in the front seat, see if you can hit Big Guy's lap the first pop. It's a real grin.

Once at the vet's office, you almost have carte blanche to do whatever you want. BG doesn't want to make a big deal about disciplining you in front of strangers, so you are allowed to do any of the following: lift your leg on the potted palm all vets have in their offices (or any of the other dog owners assembled there), pick a fight with a chihuahua, wrap the leash around the legs of an elderly woman and pull like hell (be not deterred by the old lady's use of the term "attorney"), bite the vet, bite the vet's assistant (if vets didn't enjoy getting bitten, they'd have been accountants), shred your medical records when nobody is looking, or eat the drapes off the waiting-room window.

In addition, here are some games for your consideration:

THE HOUSEBREAKING GAME Whatever you do, bear in mind that doing your gastro-intestinal duties indoors is infinitely more comfortable than doing the same duties outdoors on account of it gets cold out there. I mean, BG does it, right? Why not you. When you arrive at your new house, check out all the hidden corners for possible points of evacuation. Then, use them when the urge hits. Vary the spots so that he can't ever catch you in the act. If he does catch you, rush to the arms of one of his kids and cry piteously as though he's pulling your ears off. Usually works.

THE PLAY WITH YOUR FOOD GAME Again, establish quickly that the buck-a-pound dog food he buys isn't good enough for you and that you prefer human food, as in right-from-the-dinner-table. Whine and cry and carry on until you've set the precedent that you always get fed from the table during their feeding time.

A variation on this is tipping-over-the-food-dish. This works great for making sure they know you don't like the food.

If Big Guy starts getting a little testy over all of this, the time has come for you to lay some discipline on him. Remember, though, all humans believe that a dog shouldn't be punished for something unless he's caught in the act of doing it. HA! Anyway, don't get caught.

One of the best ways to get even, should you feel the need, is by pulling the old wait-until-the-Big-Guy-leaves-the-house-and-then-eat-the-sofa gambit. The old sofa probably needed replacing anyway, and this will further endear you to the Big Guy's mate who will protect you and then buy a new sofa with the money he's been saving for a double 20. Chewing hunting boots is okay—he won't beat on you for munching on hunting gear—it might "spoil the enthusiasm." Eat the coffee table, however, and your ass is grass.

Pretty quick, Big Guy will start babbling on incoherently about something he calls "yard training." This is where your problems really begin. He's going to want you to do stuff like come to him when he calls, fetch things for him (the lazy bum), learn to stand stiff when he says "whoa," and a bunch of other tricks which collectively make the Spanish Inquisition seem like a day in the country.

The best way to handle him in this situation, no matter what the command, is to roll over on your back, put your tail between your legs, and evacuate all over yourself. This will infuriate him, naturally, but since all the dog books say, "Never discipline a puppy in the heat of anger," he'll storm off and leave you alone.

Now there's a thin line between having things your way and being given away as an incorrigible. So, you've got to throw him a bone every now and again. Do things like point a robin in the backyard where he can see you do it, bring him a sock or mitten and play fetch once in awhile, or even come when he calls you about every fourth time. If you do this, he's likely to free you from his device of torture, the "check cord."

Once you're off the check cord, the horizon—quite literally—is the limit. Pick a direction that suits your fancy, and light out in a straight line. Never mind the yelling and cursing from BG. Eventually, he'll come after you, so you never have to worry about getting lost. When he catches up with you, wait until he's about 10 feet away, and then run to him, leap up on him, and give him that "where-the-hell-have-you-been" treatment. He'll love it.

Before he gets to you, though, this is your chance to get rid of that scented flea powder. Do your best to find and roll in any of the following: a three-day-old, road-killed raccoon, a skunk, a cowflop, or all of the above.

If you really want a yuk, wait until you are in season for the first time and then take off on him. Let him find you playfully nuzzling a really ugly male beagle. Good for the Big Guy's ulcer.

Eventually, you're going to have to grow up and you'll find that you really like grouse hunting and that BG isn't such a jerk after all. But first, enjoy your youth.

The Ambush

Ｗe're driving along a country road, my kid and I, and he screeches, "Dad, there's a flock of geese in that field!"

I slam on the brakes behind a ditch row and take a quick gander (pardon). The geese are about 300 yards from the road, but only about 30 yards from a creek bed that angles from where we are to where they are. Heh heh heh.

We take off the blaze orange hats we are wearing for our planned pheasant shoot, scrounge in my shell bag for some big loads, grab our guns, and slither along the creek toward the geese. Once I hear a goose hail at a passing flock and we freeze, but those birds pass over so we continue.

When we are about 80 yards away, I have the kid check them out. He crawls up the bank and peers through the grass. "Are they moving?" I ask. "Nope, haven't moved a bit," says he. Heh heh heh.

When we are even with the closest geese, we ambush 'em, charging up the creek bed, guns bristling. Over the top, lads; Pickett up Cemetary Ridge; the Light Brigade; Wellington's cavalry at Waterloo; ashore at Omaha Beach.

We stop charging when we notice that the geese are propped up with like little sticks. I turn to the kid and say, "I think we've just made very large idiots of ourselves." The kid says, "When I said they hadn't moved, I meant they hadn't breathed."

Out of the creek bed cover 50 yards away saunters a guy in camo clothes. He is grinning; 40 yards from us, he starts to laugh. At 30 yards, the poor devil is doubled over on the ground, the lanyard from his goose call wrapped around his neck.

The kid and I slowly back away into the creek bed and vanish.

Guides

To listen to some fellows talk, there are no hunting guides in the world worthy of them, none with what it takes to stay with these sports, and to hear some guides tell it, most hunters from the city are soft little globs of executive protoplasm, spoiled kids who got bigger but not older.

Some of the finest folks I've ever met are guides, and—without exception—they've always treated me just fine. In Wyoming a few years back, my guide was Larry Schanaman, a kid who had grown up on the Plains, was a real-life cowboy, and worked for the fine Dube Outfitters out of Buffalo.

Larry wasn't supposed to be my guide on the hunt, but my guide was late getting back from elk camp, and in the couple of hours that we waited, we became close enough that I asked Pete Dube if Larry could take me out after my antelope.

I like the way Larry laughed, and I liked the country-western music he played on his truck radio, and I liked the way he was enthusiastic about everything. Most of all, I liked talking to Larry about what it was that he was going to do with his life. Larry wanted to be a policeman. He had a college education in law enforcement, and he wanted to get a job down in Denver because he didn't see how anyone could live east of the Mississippi.

I think some guides get a little surly because the hours are long, the pay probably isn't that great, and the customers are sometimes snooty. Treating a guide like a hunting buddy puts things in perspective.

In Canada hunting geese with my son, Chris, our Cree guide spoke almost no English. My Cree is non-existent, so we were even. But when he cupped his hand to his mouth, he sang a song to the snows and blues that even I could understand. The shooting on such hunts is sort of anticlimactic. So much effort is needed to even get there that the killing is secondary. As the guide called and watched the geese respond, I watched the guide watch the geese. His eyes held the wildness of creatures who live close to the earth. The game was between the Indian and the geese. I was a spectator, a necessary one, but only just barely.

Guides are notorious for their collective sense of humor. I once hunted a mule-deer with a guide, Bill, who was a first-class practical joker—very creative.

One time as I approached a draw, Bill motioned me down on my belly and had me crawl 100 yards up to where he knelt. When I got there, I whispered, "Where is he?" Bill whispered back, deadpan, "Where's what?" Funny? Ask Bill.

Maybe the worst guides in the world are those fellows who invite you to hunt in their state. When the two of you are contemplating a hunt, the phrases tossed around are:. . . "nothing under an eight-point" . . . "we limit out on ducks by nine, then hunt quail". . . "ninety flushes on woodcock a day" . . . "forty flushes on grouse in a morning" . . . "we try to pick the juvenile geese—better eating—but when they're this thick."

The conversations usually are centered around the numbers (staggering), the size (gigantic), or both (unbelievable). Yet, we believe them. Nowhere do we find out that the guide is remembering his best day ever and is passing that off as the norm. Yeah, maybe one day he *did* see nothing smaller than an eight-point, and maybe one day he *did* have 90 woodcock flushes, but not for a long time, brother, and not when you were within 800 miles.

Well, the guide will remember, about the time you arrive, that there *are* a lot of times when the bucks are small or not there, when the woodcock have flighted this early in other years, or when the geese flew high enough that they violate the commercial jet lanes.

Well, I can understand hedging. I can understand when the birds don't cooperate or the deer haven't moved down yet from the high country. Just give me a chance—at least give me a *choice*, preferably before I get there.

Will it make a difference? Would it to you? No, we'll still go, because maybe *this* is the time the 90 woodcock, low-flying geese, and big bucks all decide to return for an encore. And if we're there, we've got a chance. Besides, wouldn't you *really* rather hear the lies?

Wild Geese

Each spring, I look for them, the first skeins of Canadas coming up from the south. They stay over for a few days or weeks near my home, resting and visiting and making their plans. For the time they are here, I watch them—these proud, strong birds headed for places no human can survive for very long, to the part of the world where snow and ice are always a few degrees away.

I don't watch them as I do in the fall when I am a hunter; I watch them now in wonder. Nothing created by the mind of man comes close to the wild goose. He flies an unblemished sky, following a course passed to him from ancestors, who got it from theirs.

I can hear them talking about these things on a clear night as they pass against the moon. Humans and their trifling civilization below are a passing whim of nature, a mistake in the evolutionary time line which will be erased some spring; some spring the stacks below won't vomit up their poison and the humans will be gone, and they will inherit again what is rightfully theirs.

I can hear them singing songs to each other to keep their spirits up. I hear them telling stories as old as the earth, as they follow a path as old as time.

The Fanatic's Guide to Messing With Guns

Back when a buck was still 69¢ instead of the quarter it is today, I was content to shoot one gun. I read all the literature about how a guy shoots one gun better than the fella with a closet full of locks, stocks, and barrels.

I was happy then. I'm not happy now. Let me tell you about it.

When you start reading gun literature, one of the things that the people who write this stuff constantly tell you is that a gun will be like an extension of your mind provided the stock is "fit" to you. That means the thing has a stock on it that more or less compensates for the shortcomings Mother Nature perpetrated on you: curved spines, arms that are too long/short, necks ditto, and so forth. Get a fitted stock, they say, and hits are automatic. Grouse, woodcock, quail, you name it and the old custom gun'll do it, by Gory.

Like a sap, I swallowed this garbage and had a stock whittled for the pump I was shooting. The gunsmith told me, however, that having a custom stock made for a pump was a whole lot like putting petticoats on a lady of the evening—sure it dresses it up, but so what?

What I'd really ought to have, he says, is a side-by-side 20-gauge double. Yessir, here is the REAL all-around gun: two chokes, good handling, you name it.

Naturally, I tumble and buy the model he suggests (which he just happens to have on hand). Well, I didn't shoot all that great with it because—(drum roll)—it didn't have a custom stock. So, at a price that brought a flush to my face, I got one of those, too.

Well, I did all right with it, nothing to write home, as they used to say, about. Then I ran into a guy in the gun business who told me that doubles were okay, but that each was such a masterpiece that they were intended for certain, specific jobs, that each double should be used for certain game species only, further subcategorized into game species under certain conditions. Naturally, this all sounds plausible, so again, I tumble.

I start collecting. Pretty quick, I had early-season woodcock guns, late-season woodcock guns, early-season grouse guns, late-season grouse guns, the same for pheasants and quail.

Still, this wasn't enough. I was told that to make each piece exactly right, I had to vary barrel length, weight, choke configurations, gauge, stock fit (early-season grouse go out low and fast, later on they fly higher, thus the stocks had to be low shooting on the early gun, high shooting on the late gun), forearm types (splinter, beavertail, semi-beavertail, semi-splinter), rib types, bead types, straight grips/pistol grips/semi-pistol grips, Aghhhahhh!!!

Anyway, it gets so you can make yourself crazy; you end up doing things like trying to decide which is your rainy-day-early-season-thick-cover-close-range-over-a-setter quail gun.

Then, it came to my attention that in the business of making, selling, buying, and hiding from your wife all these shotguns, there's a grade of gun, virtually handmade, that comes from London called the "Best" gun, and eventually, you'll want one. With such a gun, you'll only *need* one, and we're back to *square* one.

The Best Gun is the highest form of the gunmaker's science and art and costs what a really nice house used to cost not too long ago. Americans are fine prospects for the firms of Purdey, Boss, Creener, and some others, and every year, more of these light game guns are made for Colonists than for Britons (who are lately, by the way, showing marked preference for Japanese over/unders, I'm told).

But the Best Gun is something, frankly, that you'd have to have rocks in your head to hunt with. I know, guns are built to be used, but on a $25,000 shotgun, a zipper scar from your gun case is worth two-hundred bucks. So, most Best Guns are left home to gather dust and value while the guilty hunt with something else, like a rainy-day-early-season-thick-cover . . .

The quest, now, becomes not to own and use a Best Gun so that it will replace all of those others we've collected, but instead to own a Best Gun so that . . . well, so that you have one.

Now comes a whole new set of problems. To buy a new gun, we have to sell old guns. We can't sell old guns, because these are the ones we're going to *use*—remember the zipper scar? The magic of a Best Gun is not in using, but in possessing, and the possessing is nearly impossible.

So, what do we do? We can't afford a Best Gun, but anything less is not good enough.

A friend of mine, Dr. Jim Hall of Traverse City, Michigan, is a fine grouse shot, keen dog man, and a nationally recognized leader in conservation movements. Jim (by the way, his son, another Dr. Jim Hall, lived with Corey Ford at Dartmouth years back and became the model for the Doc Hall of "Lower Forty" fame) could easily afford fine guns, has some, and shoots grouse with a Model 37 Ithaca pump on which the blueing is but a memory. He shoots it the "best," so that's the one he takes out. That's his grouse gun.

Maybe, here is the answer; maybe the ticket is to shoot the gun—the one gun—you like "best" and forget the obsession for possession.

I tried it. I looked at all the arguments *for* a London Best and weighed them in light of my own situation:

. . . "A Best Gun will handle a terrific pounding of a large number of shells." (I shoot maybe six boxes a year.)

. . . "A Best Gun fits your physical dimensions." (I once weighed 200 pounds; I now weigh 150. I've had knee, ankle, and eye surgery; I grew two inches after I was 21, and my spine is curving. Which physical dimensions are they going to fit?)

. . . "A Best Gun is the highest form of the gunmaker's art." (But I'm not the highest form of shotgunning life—not even close.)

Well, I don't have a Best Gun, and I won't ever have a Best Gun. And there's a simple reason for it. It was there all along, so plain I'm ashamed I didn't see it before.

I don't deserve one; if *I* were a gun, *I'd* be a Model 37 pump with the blueing off.

I wonder what Doc Hall will take for his.

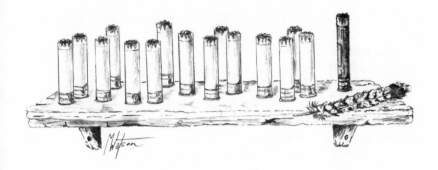

The Streak

I'm absolutely and completely sure when The Streak started. It was the tag-end of Michigan's grouse and woodcock season. I had been shooting well, but not anything to get the vapors over.

Still, my pup had come into it enough that I wasn't constantly dog training and could concentrate on what I had come out to do—shoot some birds.

I was hunting with my pal Harvey when The Streak started. We got into a flight of woodcock—mostly quick-flying males—and I got all the chances. Harvey only got to shoot his gun once, and he missed. I chortled. I had four birds with four right barrels, and I suggested heading for the car. Harvey says, "Why don't we hunt that little patch of cover over there on the way back? It'd be a shame if you had to go home without your limit (of five.)" The sarcasm's thicker than fungus on an oak log.

Naturally, I agree and my pup nails a woodcock. On a tough crossing shot at thirty-five yards, I grass the final bird. Five-for-five. It had started. The Streak.

On the way home, I explained to Harvey in detail how I had hit each shot, throwing in my theories on wingshooting, points of choke, and gun-weight hypotheses. Harvey, as is his manner, was unimpressed. Spoilsport.

The next Saturday, I was out with another pal, Crazy Artie. This time, I took four woodcock and a grouse with five shots. Artie got some exercise. The Streak stood at ten birds with ten shells. The empties on the mantle piece looked at me all week. I was starting to sweat. The news of The Streak was spreading among the grouse and woodcock hunters in town, and I was getting calls in the middle of the night. Cute little calls like: "Think you're a hotshot, huh? You gotta be shootin' 'em settin'." These were thrown at me through clenched teeth. (I suppose the ad I took out in the newspaper announcing my 10-for-10 wasn't such a good idea.)

The following week was the next to the last day of the season before it closed up for deer season (deer hunters in Michigan, like everywhere else, are Sacred Cows not to be trifled with).

I was out with Donnie, my pal who travels a lot, shoots lousy, but has a pretty good dog. Donnie and I are working a grouse cover because the woodcock are gone. Donnie gets one bird, I get five—with five shots. Donnie is convinced I'm a legend. I am now calling pals from out-of-state to tell them what The Streak is up to. Most of them hang up on me.

I figure I've got one more hunt left, the first day of the December reopener. (I don't hunt once the snow gets on the ground. Grouse have enough problems getting through the rough stuff without my adding to them.)

It's a flawless day. Donnie picks me up and we head out. The weather is like October. His dog is working beautifully. I am determined not to shoot. I mean, I'm 15-for-15. Gulp. I don't want to go, I want the season to end that way. No dice.

The birds are scarce, probably having been reshuffled by the deer hunters. Along about noon, Donnie's Britt nails a grouse next to a little clearing. I am shooting a sweet little Bernardelli 28 gauge, not the gun I used during The Streak. I tell Donnie that it's okay to miss with this gun and not have it affect The Streak because it's a different gun. Donnie says that's a damned lie and I know it. He's right, of course, but I had to try.

Anyhow, out goes the grouse in front of Donnie, about fifteen yards to his right, and he's at least fifteen yards to my right, so the bird is like thirty yards from me.

Donnie dumps both tubes at the bird and misses, as is his custom. The grouse cuts high and heads away. I draw down on him with the 28 and he tops the aspens, forty-five yards out and carrying it hard. My mind tells me, "no" just as I pull the front trigger.

There are certain creatures on this orb, certain individuals of a species who are destined not to survive. This bird is one. With a single 7½ pellet in the head, the bird collapses.

Donnie, marking the bird, sends his dog for the retrieve.

I turn and run—run, I tell you—fifteen yards away from where the bird hit the ground. Donnie takes the bird from his dog and turns to me just as I resettle, open the 28, and have the empty kick out.

He looks at me, turns and looks at where the bird hit, and I, without a word, start pacing off the distance. Sixty-one yards, I tell him casually. Not bad. But, what do you expect from a shooter on A Streak?

So, the season ends for me with sixteen birds with sixteen shots. Already, I'm getting calls from guys who want me to open the season with them next fall. I decline.

If you come to my house just about anytime between now and the next Ice Age, you'll see, set in a box of latex, fifteen twenty-gauge shells and one lone 28.

Socks

When I was in school, I woke up long enough in a psychology class to hear the professor talking about something he called "closure."

Closure, it turns out, is the feeling that a human has for wanting things to be complete; to come full circle. Finished.

It is closure that gives you and me fits as we wait for the other shoe to drop, or makes us gnash our teeth when somebody starts writing on a chalkboard without completely erasing it first.

One day, not long ago, I finally experienced the peace and contentment that can come when closure is satisfied. Let me tell you about it.

When I was about six or seven, I had a little old beagle puppy named Socks. Socks and I were inseparable buddies for the half year he was with me. He used to sleep at the foot of my bed and the last thing I felt at night and the first thing I felt again in the morning was his warm, wiggly form. I loved him with a love that has dimmed little as the years have passed.

One day, Socks turned up missing. There was a neighborhood rumor about someone being seen coaxing him into a car, but nothing could ever be proved.

Well, Socks stayed missing, and I cried myself to sleep for a lot of nights. If you've never lost a dog, then you don't know the feeling, but believe me, it only slightly diminishes with time. My parents tried everything to get me to brighten up, with no apparent luck. Maturity and years healed the wound so it no longer festered openly, just sort of scabbed over. Waiting.

Not long ago, the scab broke open. My family and I were visiting my parents at their wooded acreage in northern Michigan when the tagalong family beagle, Buckshot, turned up missing.

Now, Old Buck is a pretty good hound. He doesn't chase deer or anything like that. He resembles a big, lovable bear cub more than he does a beagle, and this day he decided to see what was on the other side of the mountain.

The problem is, I've got a seven-year-old boy who figures that Buck is his personal property. The other kids are fond of the dog too, but not like Chris.

This boy is the archtypical freckled-faced little guy with missing teeth and chubby cheeks. He also has the knack of looking sad and pitiful even when he's happy. When he's broken-hearted, angels hold their breath.

Well, Chris figured his pal was gone forever, and looking at him, I could feel the years peel away. I could see myself and Socks all over again. The old pain coming back.

The rain started to fall softly as I hoisted myself into my Jeep and began driving back roads, stopping to call the dog with a disturbing touch of frenzy in my voice. In my mind's eye, I could see Chris back at the cabin, waiting with falling hopes, out in the rain wearing a slicker that was way too big.

Miles later, and with a throat scraped raw from screaming, I still hadn't reduced the family pet to possession. Driving back to the cabin, I took off on foot, avoiding Chris' eyes,
not wanting to admit that maybe a city-bred dog *could* get
turned around in all that wilderness.

I struck out for the depths of a quaint little piece of real
estate the locals refer to as "Deadman's Swamp," muttering
under my breath about beagles and their hold on small boys.
If you've ever wandered around alone 'way back in the
woods as nightfall is setting in, then you know what kinds of
tricks your mind can play on you. I felt my vision fog up. The
Big Hurt was resurfacing.

After five miles of walking and screaming and running
and sweating, I finally sat down on a slab of rock near an
open meadow and tried to sort out how I was going to tell the
little man that lives at my house that I couldn't find his dog.

From behind me, I heard a rustle. Whipping around, I
saw Old Buck bounding up to me with that where-the-hell-
have-you-been attitude that runaway dogs muster up when
they're finally found. We rolled on the ground together, my
frustration and dismay dissolving in the wet ferns. After a
bit, I put the dog at heel and we half stumbled and half ran
back to the cabin.

When we came out of the woods, my own father, my son
with the long face, and the vagabond beagle grabbed and
hugged one another. This is when it hit me, this closure.

I felt disembodied; I was suddenly an outsider. More
than that, I felt as if I weren't even there at that spot. Instead,
I was transported back in time to witness a homecoming I'd
hoped for, but never experienced.

My Dad was still there, trim and fit despite his years, and
looking 30 again. The little boy hugging the spotted hound
was me—a quarter century ago. And Old Buck? He was another, now long-dead beagle who'd finally found his way
back. Socks had come home.

Things I'd Do

I f I had the chance, the time, or the willpower and didn't depend upon more talented friends to do things for me while I offered whiskey and admiration, there'd be lots of things I'd do. Not for any particular reason, mind you, just for the hell of it and to say I could. Maybe to show off a bit or to impress somebody before he got a chance to really know me.

I'd memorize *Gunga Din* past the part where Kipling says: ". . . and you'll lick the bloomin' boots of him what's got it."

I'd memorize Robert Service's *Spell of the Yukon* beyond the title . . . I'd learn to carve a decoy without opening a rather important artery . . . I'd learn to put the finish on a gunstock so that it would last through more than two heavy dews or one light drizzle . . . I'd really teach my setters to backpoint instead of making up excuses for them . . . I'd quit making gun trades that I'm sorry for 30 seconds later . . . I'd remember the punch lines to more than two good jokes to tell the guys at duck camp . . .

I'd go back in time to a simpler, gentler age when the closest bird coverts were within walking distance, and the pull of places like Africa and Asia weren't fraught with the dangers of international geopolitics. I'd like to be there when the steamers docked from the Continent or England and the makings of a six-month safari were unloaded and you could almost smell the cordite from the big express rifles. I'd like to be there to tag along with Ruark or Hemingway or Bell to see if I had what it takes to face down a rhino, and I'd like to go to bed wondering if a lion would tiptoe into my tent for a late night snack.

I'd do some other things, too, if I had it to do over. I'd remember that in stud poker if you have nothing by the fourth card, fold;

I'd remember that the last place to pack the Rolaids is in my gear stowed out of reach on a bush plane;

I'd remember that dogs behave in inverse proportion to the amount of bragging you do on them;

I'd remember that shooting averages do the same, and so do things like duck and goose calls, turkey calls, and plains rifles;

I'd remember that the big ugly bird dog that looks like he bites probably does, and the nice, sweet little one probably does, too;

I'd remember that Scotch does to me about what a good left hook does, and usually with the same speed;

I'd remember that "half-a-mile" to a western guide is sort of like from Moline to Wichita;

I'd remember that if I want shells in any size other than #2 12's, I'd better take them myself, and the words "sixteen gauge" might as well be "gyzlub porcridum" to a Maine storekeeper.

Last, I'd remember that bulls in pastures: a.) never die; b.) are faster than your average NFL cornerback; c.) are not, strictly speaking, vegetarians.

The Shooting Diary

The Shooting Diary. On whose yellowed pages the results of days afield are recorded, to be looked at, read, and enjoyed as time dims even the most perfect memory.

Those who gun have come to know, in ever-growing numbers, the thrill of a good log, one which points out those things that we save to savor later, perhaps with a grouse-fan feather as a bookmark. In those pages rest the records of our highs and lows afield, the "productives" by a perhaps now-dead setter, and remarks about the weather, the woodcock flights, whether the ducks we took were local birds or big, red-legged northerners pushed down ahead of the season's first squall.

Pardon me if I carry on a bit, but you see just as no man is a king to his valet, no man is a schmuck in the pages of his own shooting diary.

The entries found in *my* shooting log show an amazing ability to dodge or color the truth. Later, as memory dims, the pages take on the ring of complete truth, and I can even start to remember in my mind's eye the way the events happened according to The Book, not according to the polygraph.

For example, I have an entry dated "25 September, 1975" and the log reads like so:

> *My new pup showed quite a bit of spunk and range today. I was surprised at his stamina as well, and feel that, properly channeled, his enthusiasm will make him a real cracker-jack grouse dog.*

Now, there are a few key words here, among them: "spunk," "range," "enthusiasm," "stamina," and the phrase, "properly channeled." As I remember it, that pup had the range of a cruise missile and the speed to match. I turned him loose about eight in the morning and picked him up in the next county along about nightfall. As far as spunk goes, he picked a fight with my hunting partner's docile, 11-year-old setter bitch in the back of the car on the way to the covert. "Stamina" comes from his ability to outrun not only me but the car I was driving trying to catch up to him. "Properly channeled" has something to do with an electric shock collar and enough juice to brown-out Pittsburgh.

Here's another entry, this time while I was duck hunting:

> *Charlie and I on the Bay taking northern birds flying strongly ahead of a spanking wind. Charlie handled all the calling today. I used the old Model 12 and really picked my shots carefully.*

Sure, Charlie handled the calling. He took my call away from me as soon as he saw I had one and threw the thing about 200 feet behind the blind into the cattails. I picked my shots carefully because I forgot to clean the gun from the last trip to a salt marsh, and the magazine tube was corroded shut, meaning I had a single shot. But, see, according to the diary, I'm a real sport, out there to enjoy the great outdoors.

Want another example? Well, I'll give you one anyhow. The Log sayeth:

Jerry and I hunting the woodcock flights. I limited out, but Jerry was unable to take a bird. This proves that I've developed into a superior shot.

Translation: I locked Jerry's gun in the trunk and then claimed I'd lost the key—my gun was in a take-down case in the back seat where I always carry it when I'm going hunting. I made this "discovery" about the key after we were 100 miles from home and ready to hunt. As long as we were there, *we* might as well let *me* hunt, right, Jer?

Here's another:

Testing a new load for Winchester today, formulating opinions on workable, useable pattern spread and penetration in normal upland situations. Once the data are all in from these tests, I'll send them my unsolicited comments and observations, but right now, my preliminary findings indicate that there is some problem in quality control concerning shot clumping and marginal fringe-hit benefits.

Yeah, you're right. Missed all day.

Wrong Place, Wrong Time

There are quite a few ways that you can mess up a hunting trip. Between us, we've probably done all of them. But, for any first-timers out there, I'm going to make it easy on you and give you some thoughts on the subject so that you don't have to go through all that trial-and-error nonsense.

Try and arrange the meager vacation time from work that you've saved for hunting so that it coincides with the long-range weather predictions and/or the *Farmer's Almanac*, both of which will call for monsoons to commence and end with your vacation.

Make sure that you always call ahead to a place where you are headed for woodcock so that the guide can tell you, "Well, they were here this evening. Whether they'll be here next week when you come is another matter. I'd say it's up to you."

Make sure that you always stand between a pointed covey of quail and the closest thick brush because the birds will *have* to fly away from you and into the open.

Make sure that all the important stuff for a duck-hunting trip—calls, licenses, thermos and so forth—is in one bag. That way, it's easier to forget/misplace/lose everything all at once and you won't end up spending a lot of time forgetting/misplacing/losing stuff a little at a time.

Make sure that the only people your dog hates and will bite—every time and on sight—are Customs Agents.

Make sure you always bet the new guy—the one with the matched pair of Purdeys—that you can outshoot him on grouse, because anyone who dresses that nicely and has guns that expensive *has* to have *some* weakness.

Make sure that the fastest route out of town on opening day passes right by your boss' house after you've called in sick.

Once, Gene Hill and I were somewhere doing something or other, and a young lass approached us. Recognizing Hill, she stepped up to him and started asking him questions about the outdoors, explaining along the way why it was that she loved it so and what she got out of what she called the "outdoor experience."

"And what about you," she finally asked Hilly. "What, to you is the very essence of the outdoor experience?"

Hill paused for a bit and pondered, sort of rolling the question around on his tongue so he was sure he had a handle on it. Finally, he looked at the young lady and she leaned forward, ready to drink in his answer.

"I think," he said, "it's being in deep water in short boots."

November

Robert Service wrote these lines: "I've clinched and closed with the naked North, I've learned to defy and defend. Shoulder to shoulder we have fought it out; But the wild must win in the end."

I've always kind of liked that little stanza, because it reminds me so much of November, an orphan among months.

November reduces humans to the bare necessities. Our plastic-tiled, computerized, electronic womb seems so fragile when compared to the onslaught and ferocity of a November gale, the kind that sinks ore freighters and snuffs out a city's power like a child blows out a birthday candle.

November will lull you to sleep with a few autumn-like days, then when you've taken the bait, it slaps you one with a haymaker and you're looking at a foot of snow or watching the branches snap off trees like toothpicks tossed aside by a boisterous and brawling giant.

November reminds us that we spent the fall hunting and we don't have enough firewood, didn't put up the storm windows, and forgot to clean out the garage enough to get the car inside.

But there is a primeval beauty in November, a strange kind of melody in a first-of-the-year blizzard, if we'll only listen. November sings us a song about being puny, insignificant, and not all that independent, compared to the might of its howling gasps.

November reminds us who listen that we are, after all, only humans who won't pass this way again. November tells us that it was here first and will be here when we have gone.

This November, listen to the song, and try to feel small. It's good for us strutting humans to feel small next to nature once in every while. November can turn that trick for us in a single evening, if we'll only listen.

The Meeting

I saw him coming a long way off, sort of bouncing along as if just being there was pleasure enough. I could see that our paths were going to converge where the strip of knocked-over corn he was working shared a border with the alder swale I was pushing.

Knowing there was no way to avoid him, I waited by the old fencepost for him to come out of the corn. When he saw me he slid open the action of his pump, then ambled over. I had my double broken, dangling in the crook of my arm.

His nondescript hound and my setter took an immediate liking to each other, thankfully. There's nothing like a really good dog fight to get two strangers to agree to remain strangers.

I noted the bulge in his gamebag, and he produced an October-fat rooster pheasant. I showed him my two woodcock. "Yeah," he said, "I heard you shoot a couple of times. So those are woodcock, huh? Well, you can have 'em. Seems like a lot of effort for not too much meat."

He laughed as he said it, and I had to agree with him. Compared to his chunky cockbird, there really wasn't much meat on a woodcock—even two woodcock.

I allowed as how I didn't hunt pheasants much anymore—preferring ruffed grouse and woodcock with a sweet-breathed little setter to help me pass the hours and the miles.

At the mention of the word grouse he threw back his head and laughed. "Mister, you can have my share of all the grouse on this earth; I flat out can't hit'em."

I told him that wasn't going to make him any points if he was looking for some exclusive title—nobody can hit them regularly. Besides, I added, I had heard his 12-gauge boom only once, and that equalled one pheasant, so things had to be going pretty well for him.

He accepted the left-handed compliment with a nod. He told me he worked the third shift at an auto plant and that back home with his three kids was a good woman who knew how to fix pheasants. I told him I had three kids back home, too, none liking woodcock, and so I never shot more than a couple just for myself, and I fixed those myself.

I told him my recipe: frying the breasts in onion to take the wild taste out a bit. In fact, I said, I had a few woodcock home in the freezer, and so he was welcome to give these a try. I handed him the birds and he took them, thanking me. He started to hand me his pheasant but I quickly added, "Woodcock go especially well when they're panfried with pheasant."

He looked at me and smiled with his eyes.

We talked a bit longer. I asked him how his hound handled running pheasants, and he wanted to know if I could get my setter to strike a point for him because he'd never really seen it before. Luckily, my dog remembered her training and froze on my "whoa." He said that a man could get really used to seeing such a fine dog do such a fine thing with birds. I remarked that the proof was in the pudding and that his rawboned male was a proven producer.

Then we made those, "Well, looks like we're losin' the sun" noises and drifted apart—he into his cornfield and his pheasants and I to my alder swale and my woodcock.

I've looked for him there on other hunts, in that place where the alders meet the corn, but I haven't seen him since, haven't heard his 12 make it's flat, hollow-sounding boom. But every time I hunt that cover, I'll look for my friend whose name I never learned.

We'll meet again, I hope, he pausing in the pursuit of pheasants, and I dawdling away a little time out of woodcock cover. Perhaps for another quarter of an hour, as at our first meeting, all else won't matter—only the fact that two men sharing something in common can stand together in the October sun.

Kids

Doc, a friend of mine from Pennsylvania, called me the other day with a little story he thought I'd like.

Seems his young son was going to hunt deer for the first time, and all that summer Doc had taught the kid everything there was about waiting patiently on a stand, keeping the wind right, safety, ballistics, windage, elevation, leading on a running deer, and so forth.

Especially safety—he just drummed it into the kid's head. Be careful! Know your target! Ad nauseum, Doc deduced from the kid's attitude. Enough, already, Dad!

Well, the afternoon before opening day, they were driving to their camp and Doc was hammering on the kid some more about safety. There was a long lull in the conversation after awhile, and the kid, with a twinkle in his eye, pointed to a plaster model of a Holstein cow in front of an ice cream store and said in an excited voice, "Wow, Dad, I sure hope I get a shot at a deer like *that*!"

Doc figures the kid will be ungrounded sometime within the next three administrations.

For Keeps

In what passes for the place I keep my stuff—I call it my "den," the rest of the house calls it "the place he keeps his stuff"—is a rather motley collection of slickers and parkas and decoy anchors and waders that leak someplace or other, and I spend a lot of time sorting the stuff out in the late summer.

Part of the sorting process is also the sorting out of the mind. Memories are retrieved for another look, and eventually I end up pawing through the old trunk that I keep the memories in. I'm sure you have a special place like this, full of odds and ends that don't have any value or meaning to anyone but you.

On top of the pile is a photograph of Gene Hill and me at the Orvis Sporting Clays shoot a couple years ago. It shows

Hill in a pit blind ready to shoot the "incoming mallard" station, and I'm bending over giving him some advice on how to hit those targets. I hadn't shot yet, so I was free to give out free advice. The look on Hilly's face is what you'd expect, the same look he gives me when I give him advice on how to shoot woodcock.

Below the photo is a drake mallard curl stuck into a 20-gauge steel shotsell, empty, and taped on the shell is a message: "First duck, Chris Smith, October, 1984."

Charlie Lichon and I took my 12-year-old son out for his first shoot that year, and he shot a fine drake just at sundown. Even though it was October, it started to snow and it snowed horizontal most of the day and the birds weren't working. Finally, Charlie called in a single and Chris dropped it and Charlie's fat Lab, Jill, made the retrieve and then we picked up and left. Funny, I don't remember my first duck, but I remember that one.

There's a nondescript 12-gauge shell in there that I think came from the first, last, and only Scotch double I ever shot. Two pintail drakes were crossing as they decoyed, and I shot at one and they both fell. Sheer luck, and I spent the rest of the day pointing out to my pal, John Stevens, how experienced duck shots like myself can do that when we want to and the reason I don't do it more often is because I don't want to.

The trunk also holds the usual assortment of decoys with broken heads and the registration sticker that I was going to put on my old duck boat but Curt Campbell burned the boat because I told his wife how much his dozen Mason Decoys were worth one time and she turned them into hall carpeting and a sofa.

There's a whole set of photos of Charlie and Chris and me at a goose-hunting camp in Manitoba and we're holding up some blues and snows and looking happy as clams, and I remember how I had to really save to make that trip and it was worth every dime and more.

There's a couple of pipe stems that have teeth marks in them from where I was smoking a pipe when a surprise single tried to splash in and I took a shot with the pipe still in my mouth and the recoil made me bite damn near through to the other side. I don't know why I save those. Maybe, I figure, I'll heat up a paper clip and reopen the stems and use them again, but I'll probably just get new ones.

Lots of people including some I live with would call this stuff junk, and I guess I'd have to agree if I didn't have a certain, sharp memory attached to every little odd and end. That memory becomes tangier every time I look at that piece of the past.

And how about you? Have you got your first, or biggest, or prettiest grouse fan? How about drake curls, many or maybe just your first, or maybe three for the time you made that triple? I wish I could have seen your face, I'll bet you whooped and laughed, and relived the shots to your pals a dozen times before they finally begged for silence.

Where do you keep the tarnished .30-30 shell you used on your first buck? Do you take it out and polish it every couple of years? Do you keep it near the picture of your father and you hauling the deer out of the woods? Hard to tell who was prouder, isn't it?

We keep our memories in the same places we bury dogs and pals who are no longer with us. We keep these treasures in the vaults that hold the sights of geese pitching into a set of field decoys and quail buzzing out of a brushy corner by a split-rail fence.

And when the time comes when it's easier to remember old times than to gather up new ones, it is to this place that we go, you and I, to watch for the last flight at sunset. I'll meet you there.

Some Of My Best Friends

There are a few people I know really well, and unlike most friends, I always get to visit these friends when they're at their best.

One of my best friends is William Harnden Foster. He wrote *New England Grouse Shooting*, and I can pick up his work and find his words as timely and as meaningful as they were when he wrote them just for me back in the 40's.

Another pal is Havilah Babcock, the old professor, who spent a lot of his time chasing quail all over the South. Whenever I sit down to visit with him, he's always in rare form. Still another is my good friend Colonel Jim Corbett, who spent so many years haunting the hill country of India. His *Maneaters of Kumaon* is a classic that has passed the tests of generations.

62

Even though these men are gone, their words are as fitting to us now as when they wrote them, and I guess that's how I feel about good sporting books. A glass of something to ward off the night air, a stout fire of white ash logs, and a setter crowding your feet may seem pretty trite, but it's about the closest slice of perfection most of us are likely to get in this life. Even closer to perfect, if you've got a good friend with you.

I was visiting with one of these friends the other night, reading the fine story, "Letter to a Grandson," instead of cleaning the garage like I'd promised. Typical. While I was listening to Corey Ford, it occurred to me that I'd been a little sloppy in getting my own affairs in order (God, what a morbid phrase).

In his story, Ford tells how one of the characters in his famed "Lower Forty" club, on becoming a grandfather, had sat down and written a letter to this grandson he'd not yet seen. In the letter, which the lad was to open on his 16th birthday, Ford wills the kid some of his outdoor stuff, wishes him good luck, tells him to shoot straight and to tell the truth. Great advice, beautifully written.

Well, I decided that maybe I'd ought to do the same thing. Though I'm still too young to have a grandson, I do have two boys to think of and, you never know, fate just might get even for all the stuff I've done and so far gotten away with. I sat down and wrote these words. For what they're worth, here they are:

Dear Son,

If you read this, it's because I finally got what was coming to me and I'm being paid back for all my sins, those I committed or those your mother imagined I committed, or those I committed and she doesn't know a damn thing about, all in the name of spending too much time hunting and messing with dogs and guns. Since I consider my life well lived, even though it has been cut a little shorter than I'd have liked, I'm going to give you some advice—free for nothin'.

Make sure that your wife, once you've picked her out, has

*what's called a "proper appreciation" of the outdoor pursuits. By this
I mean, get you a woman who can't add—like she can't add up your
checkbook entries or credit-card slips, so she has no idea how much
you spend on stuff. Your mother still thinks some of my guns cost
$55. Until now, I've been lucky. See that you are.*

*Make sure that you take off every Opening Day for hunting
instead of working for a living. Work will always be there—Opening
Day comes once a year.*

*Enough domestic advice. Now for the good stuff. Our house
has a number of nooks and crannies all, as my pal Gene Hill says,
"groaning with the weight of locks, stocks, and barrels." Since I've
always shot doubles, your mom never looked beyond the barrels on
any gun. She always assumed I had one shotgun. Look behind the
chimney in the attic. My matched set of Ithaca 20's is there. My
Parker 16 and Churchill 12 are wrapped up in a blanket, disassem-
bled, in the bottom of the stairwell behind the moosehead your
mother hates. That little Orvis 28 gauge is in a box inside the
humidifier box which is next to the carton of furnace filters that I
have the rat poison, roach traps, and ant powder spread around. I've
found that if you want to hide something from the missus—and
unless my genes slipped you will—put roach traps around it; sure-
fire.*

*That nice gun case that I brought back with me from Mexico—
the one I told your mother cost $9 in American money—actually
was shipped to El Paso from England where I had it made. Cost
about 50 times that much. I picked it up after a dove shoot once.
You'll find that and the L.C. Smith 16 gauge I keep in it stored in
the false ceiling above my clothes closet. Take it down carefully
because the Smith is in beautiful shape—never fired. I got it by . . .
well, do you remember the time that I was away on business and I
called home for money to fix the car? Well, there hadn't been a
breakdown. But there was this Smith and . . . anyhow, that's how I
got it.*

*If the people from the bank come to see the new bathroom and
recreation room they've financed, you may as well show them the
Powell 16 gauge—that's what they paid for.*

*One little story—I think you're old enough—will point out how
careful you have to be. Seems once a man let his emotions run away*

with him and a beautiful young secretary was "available." One thing led to another, and soon the man was "compromised." On his way home, he stopped at a gun shop and bought some Hoppe's #9 and rubbed it on his hands.

Entering his house, he found his wife waiting, glaring at him. "Where have you been?" she screamed. "Dear," said the man, "I got carried away with a new secretary, one thing led to another, and I was unfaithful to you. Please forgive me."

The man's wife reached out, grabbed his hand, lifted it to her face, and smelled it.

"If only it were that simple," she said, "but it's not—you bought another gun!"

Love,
Dad

Amortization

Tom Petrie is a fellow I mention elsewhere in this book, specifically, I tell how he gets lost a lot. Tom and I were sitting around cluttering up the kitchen in his Wisconsin farm home last winter, admiring the new litter of setter pups his Sadie and my Parker had. I told him how Parker had been insufferable, handing out cigars and all back in Michigan when he'd found out that Sadie and her seven had brightened up Christmas Eve for Tom and his sainted, patient, wife, Patti.

Tom, who is my boss at Willow Creek Press, is an astute businessman who was confiding to me, in low tones, how he planned to buy a Purdey shotgun. I told him a Purdey cost about as much as a first-born female child sold into white slavery, plus a car. Tom asked me how I knew and I told him that I'd made a good deal for my daughter, but I couldn't bear to part with my car and that's how come I didn't have a Purdey myself.

Well, Tom explained, that's because as a lowly editor, I didn't understand the magic of what he called "amortization." I told him that it was a word I'd seen on the federal tax forms during my annual bout with perjury, but other than that, he was right and he should explain.

Tom looked at me and asked me if I like Big Macs—like the sandwich. I said I hadn't thought about it much, but I guessed so, and why. Tom said that he didn't like Big Macs, and that was how he was going to get his Purdey.

He asked how many years I figured he had left to hunt. I said at his present level of gin consumption, about a week-and-a-half.

Tom said he figured, my guess notwithstanding, about 40 years. Now, this is where the magic comes in. A $25,000 Purdey over 40 years is—amoritized—only $625 a year. That's, Tom said, about $1.75 a day—the cost of a Big Mac. And since he didn't like Big Macs, he'd take the money he'd *normally* spend on Big Macs and buy a Purdey. See?

Just then Patti walked into the kitchen, glanced at us, instantly read Tom's mind, and that was the end of that.

But, it got me to thinking about this whole Purdey-or-a-Big-Mac concept, this amortization magic of taking money that you would *normally* spend on something, spending it on something else, and stretching it over a long period of time so you can get damn near anything you want.

Now, I have always wanted to go to England and shoot driven pheasants. It would be the trip of a lifetime, but it costs a lot—too much, unless you amortize. Since I don't chew gum because I smoke a pipe, I could pay for the trip with the money I would *normally* spend on gum.

If I took 35¢ I'd *normally* spend on gum the rest of my life and went right now, had a good time, and promised to remember my trip every day of my life—instead of buying gum—the trip would be paid for through memories-instead-of-gum amortization.

What about you? Is there a gun you want? Swear off cream of octopus soup. How about a new duck boat? Give up those opera tickets you'd *normally* buy. A mule deer hunt in Wyoming? Use the money you had earmarked for your son's ballet lessons.

The possibilities are endless.

Thanks, Tom.

A Chance To Double

The calf-deep snow pulled at his boots as he followed the setter into the small, brushy stand. It hadn't been a good grouse year. The jury was still out as to why. Some said the cycle was down, others argued that the late shooting—the winter season—had a continuing harmful effect on the birds at a time when they really needed protection.

Lately, he had started to wonder if his own late-season hunting had hurt some of his own coverts. He had listened to the various arguments: "You can't shoot them out. When the numbers get low, people stop hunting grouse and they come back." "Winter hunting takes birds that are normally breeding stock. You might as well be shooting them in May as in December."

He had always trusted the biologists, those who told him that his hunting wouldn't hurt the population, that these were birds that would die anyway. But now it seemed like you could find a biologist who would tell you whatever you wanted to hear—sort of like "expert testimony" in a court of law: you get your expert and I'll get mine and, on balance, we're even.

Some of all of this had a subliminal effect on him; he didn't go out as often or hunt as long when he did. It was only through the setter's urging that he was out today at all. He was starting to wonder, starting to question. He worked hard for his birds, took them fairly and in full flight, and he loved them—loved that which he killed.

Ahead of him the bell had stopped and he snapped back to the present. He inched in, the little 20 gauge double ready. The setter was staunch, and ahead of her, a pair of grouse thundered out and cut for the next patch of cover. To get there, they had to cross open ground. That was their mistake.

His first shot was true, and the grouse puffed and fell. From the corner of his eye, he was aware that the dog had started to break and then remembered her training and held.

He recovered from the recoil of the first barrel and leveled down on the second, now lone, bird. It was an easy shot—30 yards out and quartering away. The 20's tight barrel would take the grouse easily. His first chance to double all season.

He swung past, established the lead and, at the critical moment, didn't pull the trigger. Instead, he silently uttered "Bang." A brace would have been nice, and taken as a snappy right-and-left double, even nicer. But, his personal sense of "enough" told him no—told him to spare this winter bird.

And perhaps this was the answer. Lowering his gun, he watched the bird slant into cover. He thought that if every shooter developed his own sense of enough, the arguments would be unnecessary, the point moot.

He'd had his chance to double and hadn't—by choice. To him, that was the most satisfying.

Carburetor Heads

If my years of teaching school taught me anything, they taught me that the Carburetor Heads out there will never read what I'm going to say about them, because those who end up that way never learned to read for the most part, anyhow.

Our society, with its sick, little perverse attraction to the internal combustion engine, has spawned a group of Arrested Developmentees who get their pleasure in the outdoors by tearing it up on knobby tires. I mean the dirt bikes were bad enough, but at least the Faithful like you and me could always hold out hope that the two-wheelers would flip over on the guilty, and thereby raise the local average IQ.

But now, they've got three-wheelers and four-wheelers that go just as fast and are just as loud and can rearrange, depending upon which the idiot is riding, 150–200% of the ground that a cycle used to.

Telling these people that they can't enjoy the outdoors the way they want is a little pompous, I guess, but these people are defiling that which I love and turning woodcock coverts into wastelands. The bugs-on-the-teeth, you're-beautiful-because-you're-you crew is alive and well and ripping up the earth for the sake of "getting away from it all." Think how much better they could commune with nature if they had tanks.

I once knew an oak tree, a giant white oak with branches as big as a man's waist and acorns the size of small plums. I used to visit her every hunting trip I made to her home. Luckily, she lived on public land, so nobody ever stopped me from going to see her and setting my weary carcass in her brown leaves. From the sign around her, I wasn't the only one who liked to come see her. Squirrels foraged there for acorns and built their leaf nests in her branches. Deer shuffled by and picked up acorns or just flopped down to rest in her shade. She was a big old gal, as thick through the middle as your leg is long, and not a sign of blight or heart rot on her, this old lady of mine.

A few months back, I took my son to see her. The day was overcast and rainy, but I knew her branches—holding the leaves late as oaks will do—would shelter us as we relaxed and ate our lunch.

Aldo Leopold, naturalist/grouse hunter, wrote nearly 35 years ago that you can trace the history of a woodlot or a forest by reading the signs in an old oak tree. Once occupying open pasture land, the old gal had lately taken to growing straight up through the canopy of aspen, birch, and other, lesser, trees. The lower limbs had started to shade out and no longer held leaves, but it would be years before she lost those sturdy limbs to wind or ice.

But I got to read more than I wanted in that tree of mine. I got to read her age—108 years. I know because I counted the rings on her stump, the only thing left of her. It seems some jerks figured she'd be just the ticket for a winter's supply of firewood, so they cut her down, split her up, and threw her into a truck and barreled away. That tree had been growing when the white pine was king in these parts. How many storms, blizzards, and fires she had to survive, nobody can say. She fell to the chain saw of a Saturday afternoon pioneer and a few of his cronies.

All I can do now is pray for a really good chimney fire.

A Boy's First Hunt . . .

(or, don't tell everything you know, kid)

I nosed the Jeep off the gravel road onto the blacktop. Heading east, I turned the rearview mirror up to keep the sun from reflecting into my eyes and settled back for the drive home.

My companion was my younger son, Jake. At eight years old, he had just experienced his first all-day grouse hunt with his Dear Old Dad and my hunting buddy, Mark Sutton. I'd dropped Sutton off at his house near Bay City, and we were heading home. The Jeep had considerably more room in it than when Mark and his big pointer, Packer, had been with us.

As I watched the highway stripes blend into telegraphic dots and dashes, I thought it best to start questioning Jake about the day. He had been with me on other, shorter hunts since he was six, but today marked his first full day's hunt with another person and a pointing dog. I knew he was full of questions. I prepared to give him the benefit of my knowledge.

"Well, Son," I started, "What did you think of today? Did you have fun?"

"Oh, yeah," he brightened. "It was really fun!"

I tried to open him up. "Do you have any questions? Did anything happen today that you don't understand? Dad will explain it if he can."

"Well, yeah. There ARE some things that I didn't really understand," he offered.

I let him think for a minute. I share a good relationship with all three of my children, and I knew Jake would talk when he was ready. The sun had almost set, and I swiveled the mirror back into place.

"Dad, remember when you got to the first place to hunt this morning?"

"You mean the first 'cover'?" I corrected gently.

"Yeah, the first cover. Well, why did you call Mr. Sutton's dog all those names that Mom doesn't let you say around the house?"

"Well, Son," I fidgeted, "Mr. Sutton's dog sometimes does some things right outside the Jeep door that Dad doesn't like, and today Dad put his foot in one of those things." I hoped the kid wouldn't pursue this line of questioning very long.

"Yeah, you seemed mad. You even called Mr. Sutton some of the same names when he laughed so hard. Do you always use the same names on Mr. Sutton that you do on Mr. Sutton's dog?" Jake asked.

"Not always, Son, just sometimes. Let's forget about the dog. Did you want to ask me anything else?"

"Well, remember when you were loading your gun this morning? You always taught me to keep my hand back from where the shells go in before you close it up, but you didn't do that yourself this morning. How's your thumb now, Dad?"

I'd almost forgotten the throbbing in my thumb til then.

"When Mr. Sutton laughed at you again, you called him some of those names again, didn't you Dad?" the kid was faintly smiling.

"Uh, yes I did. Let's not tell Mom. That'll be our secret, okay?" He was starting to make me nervous, and I stepped a little harder on the gas.

"I remember when Packer pointed the first grouse and you and Mr. Sutton moved in on it and you had me watch from behind and you got to shoot at the bird. I'll bet you wish you still had that gun that holds five shots because the gun you've got now with only two barrels makes it harder to hit birds with, doesn't it?"

"Well, sometimes even Dad misses both barrels," I chuckled.

"Yep, altogether, you could have used more shots about eleven different times. I was counting because I picked up the empty shells when your gun threw them out, like you told me."

"Yeah, Son," I answered, "some days you can't buy a bird. You'll find that out when you start to hunt."

"Mr. Sutton was really shooting good today. He hit all four grouse he shot at plus those two woodcock. It was sure nice of him to give you those two grouse and woodcock or we wouldn't have anything to take home to Mom for dinner. How come you called him those names because he was shooting really good, Dad? Was it because he was laughing at you when you missed?"

"Uh, yeah, Son. Mr. Sutton sometimes teases me too much about my shooting," I responded.

"Does Mr. Sutton always give you half his birds, Dad?"

I stepped down a little harder on the gas and kept silent.

"Oh, wait!" exclaimed Jake. "I remember now, you did shoot a woodcock this afternoon. Does Packer always eat woodcock like that? She doesn't eat Mr. Sutton's woodcock when HE shoots them."

"You noticed that, eh? Well, some dogs won't even touch

a woodcock. Packer loves them and usually tries to eat the first one she can. Usually, it's the one I've shot," I answered.

"You don't REALLY think Mr. Sutton trained her to do that like you said, do you, Dad? That would be really hard to train a dog to eat a bird, especially when she fetches the rest of the birds to Mr. Sutton so good." I detected a frightening streak of his mother in Jake, a streak I hadn't noticed before.

"I think the funniest part of the whole day was when Mr. Sutton's dog was in the Jeep and we were standing outside and she ate your lunch. It's a good thing that Mr. Sutton looked inside just as she was getting ready to eat his lunch. How come you said that Mr. Sutton was watching all along and waited until she ate your lunch before he said anything? Would he really do that?" Jake's big eyes were boring into the side of my head.

"Son, Mr. Sutton likes to have fun at Dad's expense. He has had fun at Dad's expense since we were both your age," I answered.

"Yeah, it was a good thing that Mom packed me a big lunch or you wouldn't have had anything to eat. That was fun eating lunch under that big tree in that cow pasture. Did you and Mr. Sutton know that the big cow was there? He really got mad at Packer, and when she ran toward us, the cow chased us too, didn't he? Dad, are all fences electric like that one?"

"No, Son, just the ones that have bulls inside," I answered.

"I'll bet that fence wouldn't have hurt you near as much when you put that one leg over if you hadn't fallen into that ditch earlier. Mr. Sutton told me that being wet makes the electricity hurt more. He sure laughed at you that time, too, Dad." The kid was grinning from ear to ear.

"Well, Son, that only proves that you've got to be careful. I should have known that the bull was still living there and that the fence was electric, but I forgot," I explained.

"Well, if that was your fault, how come you kept calling Mr. Sutton, Packer, and the bull those names while you were caught on the fence? You called another man some of those names, too, Dad. Did you really know Benjamin Franklin?"

"Never mind, Son, we're almost home. Let's make today our little secret, okay?"

As the Jeep pulled into the driveway, Sue came out the back door to greet us. Jake bailed out of the Jeep and ran toward her.

"Guess what, Mom, Daddy called Mr. Sutton and a man named Benjamin Franklin a . . ."

The Crazies

I was looking at my hunting stuff the other day, and I was struck by the amounts of money and time we spend in the pursuit of accumulation. I mean, when we aren't hunting, we are training dogs, shooting at the club, trying to wangle a new gun/dog/print/book/et cetera. If we ever put this amount of planning and time into our business affairs, we'd all be company presidents with credit cards and Lear jets, probably.

And, with the crazy season (the time that drags before the season opens) upon us, the crazies increase exponentially—as in "crazies to the third power," as opposed to merely "the crazies squared."

I was sitting around discussing this phenomenon with a couple pals of mine, Roadkill McGarrity and Fishbait Lichon, the other night. Both of these guys are avid grouse hunters, although Lichon will, on occasion, hunt waterfowl, but I let him in the house anyway because he always brings whiskey.

Roadkill says the way he gets his dose of the crazies is trying to smuggle prints into the house, ones he buys at RGS banquets or orders from galleries.

"I try to sneak the prints in past Karen, my wife, with almost no luck. She can smell the rag paper on a new print and not only gives me hell for buying it, she usually impounds the thing and it ends up on the family room wall over the ping-pong table instead of in my den where I can look at it."

"Like with me," Fishbait offers, "it's getting guns in and out that's tricky. The other day, I bring home a nice little Spanish side-by-side 20 I picked up for a few hundred—a good deal. Anyway, the Storm and Strife is waiting by the door with that FBI look in her eyes. She starts with the usual third degree about what's in the box. I tell her that this is a gun I've got on loan from Roadkill and that I'm going to refinish the stock for him because he's so ham-handed. She walks to the phone and calls Roadkill and says, 'I'm looking for Charles. Have you seen him lately?' Stupid here, figuring I'm in a jam, claims he hasn't laid eyes on me for three weeks. Adios Spanish side-by-side."

"Well," counters Roadkill, "that isn't as bad as the time I asked you to cover for me while I went to Wisconsin for three days grouse hunting. All I wanted you to do is tell anyone who asked that we had been up putting a new roof on your cabin instead of spending a fortune on an out-of-state trip. So what happens? Nutsy here (gestures toward Fishbait) calls my house the next day looking for me. When I called home from Wisconsin, the wife's voice has got ice on it."

"Yeah? What about the time you tried to hook me into going halves with you on that Model 21 Winchester you had at such a 'good deal?'" Fishbait is retaliating. "'Invest a few hundred and get back a fortune when we sell it,' you said. So I did, only you used the thing for three years, and you'd still be shooting it if I hadn't gone over to your house and taken the damn thing and sold it myself . . ."

"And kept my half of the money for three years!" Roadkill is still smarting.

Fishbait stands and his hackles are up. I say, "Well, guys . . ."

"Shaddup, Smitty," says Fishbait. "Look, McGarrity, what about all the damn shots you steal in a season? I ask you, 'Is the dog on point over there?' You say, 'Nah, haven't seen her.' Three seconds later, I hear, 'Pow, Pow.' Then I hear that stupid cackle of yours. You saw the dog the whole time and you aren't telling me."

"If I did, it wouldn't do any good. You can't hit birds anyway. If you don't have a damn Lab slapping you in the face and dead carp floating by a duck blind, you can't hit nuthin!" Now, Roadkill has not passed Go, he hasn't collected $200, he's gone directly for the jugular.

"Yeah? Well what about that batch of stuff you pass off as food at grouse camp? You think you got the name 'Roadkill' for nuthin'? Even the plates you serve that slop on have rigor mortis." Fishbait turns to me, "Did you ever notice that you never see any dead animals on the road in a five-mile radius of grouse camp? The reason is because you and I've been eatin' 'em for years."

I say, "Well, guys . . ."

"Shaddup," says Roadkill. He glares at Lichon. "You still think I didn't know it was you at last year's RGS banquet that kept upping the bid on that print I wanted? You asked me before the dinner which print I was after, so like a sap, I tell you and you keep jacking the price up, jacking it up all the time."

"It was for a good cause, Cheapskate!"

"GUYS!" I shout. They stop and look at me. I fill their glasses and raise mine up.

"Here's to the Crazies."

"Amen," they say.

J. Smith

Duck Hunters

About every other day or so, somebody will stop me on the street to ask, "Smitty, exactly what *is* a duck hunter?" Naturally, this has made me stop and think—something of a miracle—and I think I've come up with a few answers. Some of these, the guilty may not like; others, we'll have to acknowledge.

A duck hunter is a guy who is besieged with problems. Problems like dogs that retrieve dead ducks, dead geese, dead carp, dead cattails, dead decoy anchors, and your buddy's dead lunch. Problems like wives who think in terms of wallpaper and carpeting instead of pump guns and duck boats. (My own wife has even tried to sell some of my ducking stuff at a garage sale on the flimsy excuse that the kids needed school shoes. Ha!) Problems like motors that manage to break down about the time a gale that could send shivers down the spine of a Great Lakes freighter's skipper blows up. Problems like trying to lead a downwind teal far enough to connect and still keep the bird in sight over your off shoulder.

Problems like trying to break the world's record for most mud in a pair of waders by an amateur. Problems like using a hand calculator with mittens on to see if you're over the point total.

To understand these problems, we've got to understand ourselves. This can be tough. How can we or anyone else understand a person who had fun in a sneakbox boat on Lake Huron on a day that would have snuffed the *Queen Mary*?

We know, because we've been there. We've had calls freeze up and we've dropped our last shell overboard as the mallards were decoying and we've had the boat tip over on us a time or two. We've made shots, you and I, that were damn lies and missed some that were so easy that we wanted to turn the gun on ourselves.

Knowing all this, see if this doesn't sound like some folks we both know and love: A duck hunter can't remember his wife's birthday but can tell you to the minute in time his Lab was born. He forgets the Joneses are coming over for dinner but can tell you—without a calendar—what day of the week Opening Day will fall on four years from now.

He can't find his brown suit in the closet, but he can locate his favorite blind in a driving rain storm two hours before first light.

He never washes his car, but you could eat off the stock of his 870. He shrugs when gas jumps a quarter a gallon but screams blue murder when shotshells go up a nickel a box— even though his ratio of gallons to shells is about 100 to one.

He doesn't notice his wife's new hair style or dress, but he can tell you from two miles off in half light if that little flock is mostly mallards or sprigs.

Sometimes, he even gets upset. Duck hunters find it easy to hate bulldozers, subdivisions, clear skies with no wind, dry springs on the Canada potholes, pump guns that jam, cold coffee, squeaky oar locks, motors that won't start, sky shooters, loose anchor ropes, dogs that fetch decoys instead of ducks, forgetting their lunches, and the U.S. Army Corps of Engineers.

Usually, however, duck hunters are lovers. We love Labs named *Queen* and *Tar* and *Midnight*, wide-eyed boys on their first hunt, getting up at 3 A.M., old parkas and hip boots, the sound of the port slamming shut on an automatic, duck calls that actually sound like ducks (sort of), a few geese now and again, quarter-mile retrieves, sunrise singles, gales that curl your lips, the smell of a wet dog, slightly numb feet, naps between flights while the new guy keeps watch, buddies who mark the passing of years by counting the opening days, pals who say "great shot" and they're talking about you, wives who know how to cook steak and eggs at four in the morning, remembering your thermos, full chokes, a good lie, 28-inch barrels, watching the weaklings head for shore when the temperature nudges 25° below, a teenage daughter who actually likes to clean guns, and the sight of a buddy's face in the flicker of a match as he lights his pipe just before dawn.

So, what is a duck hunter? He is a combination naturalist and ornithologist; a nature lover in the finest sense because he understands. He is a man inclined toward a fistfight at the mention of "diking and draining." He loves the birds he hunts, and he loves his sport. He is Daniel Boone, U.S. Senator, Rachel Carson, infantry soldier, ban the bomb'er, amateur sailor, and card-carrying lunatic. He walks a little faster and stands a littler taller each autumn. He spends way too much money to get way too cold, way too wet, and sometimes way too lost to shoot way too few ducks.

He's us.

Dogs and Dreams

One of the things I wonder about is what dogs dream of. I wonder what moves them in their sleep to twitch their feet and curl their lips and whine and woof. Especially gun dogs; they seem to have more to dream about, maybe because they've been more places and seen and done more things worth dreaming about, maybe because they gather more to store up against the time when the season is closed or we're busy and can't go, or when age makes all days in the field only memories.

My two setters live with me. They usually plant themselves under my desk and crowd my feet while I'm trying to work, or they take turns sleeping in the good chair in my office, the one I keep covered so that if someone who wants to talk drops over, I can offer him a sort of hairless place to sit. Not that it does much good. About the time that Jess and Parker figure out the visitor is a friend worth knowing, they give him the setter welcome and his clothes look like who-finished-second in the pillow fight.

Lately, my relatives have started to talk about me and my setters. The reason is, I think, because I talk to my dogs—all the time. They hardly ever answer except to smile with their tails, but they know when I've had a bad day and try to cheer me up with a paw in the lap, a quick kiss on the cheek, or a head on the knee.

When I've had a particularly horrible day, my older dog, Jess, has been known, on occasion, to join me in a nip or two from the Company Bottle of Scotch. Jess likes a good single-malt Scotch and water and a couple of cubes to chew on after she's finished. Jess also likes bourbon, white wine, and a good, old-fashioned Old Fashion.

Last summer, Jess and I were sitting on the front porch having a sundowner or two. When we were finished, I came inside, leaving her to bask in the fading light. Three hours later, I had to go outside, carry her in, and let her sleep it off on the good chair. Next day, she spent most of the morning sniffing the drawer where I keep the Rolaids. Who says dogs are dumb animals? Not the fellow Jess drinks with. I wonder what dogs dream about when they've had too much to drink?

I wonder what dogs are doing in their dreams. Are they busting the birds joyously that they wouldn't bust, too often, when they're awake and we're watching? Do they, like we, dream of getting those things we can't get in the waking, workaday world? If a dream "is a wish your heart makes," then what do our dogs wish for?

Maybe they wish for constant October and grouse that won't run out from under a point. They wish for a hunter that hits more than one in ten pointed birds, and they wish blackberry canes had rubber thorns.

Living with gun dogs is a challenge. I'm not the type of person who puts dogs into a backyard kennel and feeds them once a day and runs them once a week. My dogs are my pals;

some days, the only ones I have. Jess, the little female, just went through a heat, which drove her nephew, Parker, wild and I had my hands full. I was beginning to think that maybe the kennel in the back wasn't such a shabby idea after all and was telling my troubles to my friend Jack Daniels when she strolled up, sniffed my glass, dropped her eyelids to half-mast, and rubbed her hip against my knee. I could swear she was giving me the setter equivalent of, "Buy me a drink, Sailor?" I did.

Once my son Chris got sick and had to take to his bed for a couple days. The dogs watched over him in shifts from the foot of his bed. Not sleeping, really, just curled up, resting, with eyes open watching him and listening to his breathing and adding the warmth of an orange-ticked body to the bed covers to ward off the chills of fever.

Although neither dog could be coaxed from the bed, they would alternate watches. Parker would walk down the hall to Chris' bedroom, give an unspoken yet understood signal to Jess who would hop off the bed while Parker hopped on. Jess would then go get a drink or take a bite or two from her dish or go outside for a stroll or come see me, and an hour later, she'd go relieve Parker. This went on day and night for three days until the antibiotics worked and the boy got better. Nothing could alter their watching and listening and changing of the guard until he was well.

I like to think that good dogs don't die in the sense that the birds they hunt die, but that they "pass on" in the human sense if you believe in that sort of thing, and I do. I like to think that a good dog is more than a memory once he's gone, that he's there with you when you train a new pup or sip a glass of whiskey by the fire, or when your boots come out of the closet on opening day.

And, I like to think one passed-on friend is there when I go to a certain cupboard in my house and stare inside at a dusty collar and bell that will never tinkle around the neck of another dog. Not ever, not even around the neck of another, living Jess who carries the same name, but not the same bell.

I know men who look on a dog as a servant to do what

he can't. These same men usually think of a fine gun as a tool, and the man/dog/gun equation is reduced to man/servant/tool. I always wonder why these people don't save their money and just buy the supermarket grouse some folks call "chicken."

Not long ago, a wealthy man from another state called because he had hunted with a mutual friend who had gotten to telling tales about Jess and how she'd handled grouse and woodcock the one time he'd hunted with us. The caller said he certainly would like to have such a dog, and I thought he was going to ask to be put on a waiting list for a puppy when he outright asked how much I'd take for her.

Well, I said I didn't know, and maybe she wasn't what he wanted, so I suggested a trial period. He asked what I meant, and I said that I'd send him Jess, and he could send me his wife and we'd each try the other's female for a couple weeks and if either didn't like the way things were going, then the deal was off.

The next sound I heard was the dial tone.

We know, you and I, that we overlook faults in dogs that we sure wouldn't tolerate in friends or blood relatives. But then, that's fair because the dogs overlook the faults we have that no one else has ever ignored, *least* of all relatives.

We'll look the other way when the dog bumps birds, claiming that scenting is wrong or the wind shifted; we pretend we don't see a mauled bird the dog retrieves, blaming instead the wrong shot size and tight chokes; we even make do with dogs that won't hold a point, bragging to friends about the keenness our dogs show.

I wonder what the state of international geopolitics and family relationships would be like if people treated people like some of us people treat our dogs.

The Rhino

I can remember, vividly, my grade-school days. It was then that the hunting bug bit me pretty good. My dad and his cronies always had good dogs and nice guns and were forever heading someplace exotic to hunt—places like Nebraska and New Brunswick. In fact, the only time I ever paid attention in geography class was when the Old Man was off chasing birds in some place that the fates had determined I learn about. I sure spent more time wondering about where he was and what he was doing than I did worrying about the GNP of Peru.

All of that was before I ran afoul of Sister Angela Rhinocerous.

The Rhino was my sixth-grade teacher. She wore the habit that hung to the floor and a crucifix that you could have used if you were a Mafia chieftain and wanted to hide one of your transgressions in the East River.

She also carried THE RULER. All of us kids—especially the boys—lived in numbing, mindless terror of The Ruler. It was half-a-yard long and it went with her everywhere. It probably even went with her to the bathroom, although it never occurred to any of us that a nun would go to the bathroom, with or without a ruler. I have wondered off and on over the decades how The Rhino got them to make her a ruler out of granite.

When she caught you in the act of something—real or the product of her vivid and active imagination—she would calmly ask you to come to the front of the room to "get your knuckles measured." To this day, the word "measured" gives me the urge to go to the john.

Anyway, the guilty would shuffle to the front of the classroom and hold out his hand—*hands* if he were *really* in trouble. The Rhino would then bring The Ruler down across his paws with a technique a little like what John Henry must have used to beat the steam drill in the spike-driving contest. Having your knuckles measured was a lot like slamming them in the car door about the time it left town.

After you got measured, you had to cry. That wasn't really a problem because right after you got your breath back, crying was sort of automatic. But if you wanted to feel like a tough guy and hoped to John Wayne your way through, forget it.

I remember Artie Nitzenbaum trying that once. He'd been shooting paper wads at Mary Kay Kazmerick, the class pet. The Rhino caught him dirty and invited him up front. She told him to produce the offending hand, and Artie held out his right hand, his eyes squinting with determination. The Rhino teed off on him, and Artie didn't even flinch. That was about as smart as wearing a red shirt to feed the cows, and The Rhino let him have it again—and again—and again. Artie broke about the time the Rhino's arm gave out.

We called Artie "Lefty" until some time after Christmas.

Now one time I was having a nice little chat with Bernard

Koviack about how I was going to go woodcock hunting with the Old Man during the coming weekend. Unfortunately, I was having the chat during arithmetic class, and the Rhino was trying to teach us how to reduce fractions. She caught me, ordered me front and center, and reduced my knuckles to a fraction of what they'd been just seconds before.

I decided to rebel. It was time to throw off the chains; to overthrow The Rhino.

Crazy Timmy O'Reilly was the class woodsman. He ran a rather ineffective trapline on his farm and always smelled like a deceased beaver. I enlisted his aid. Timmy got measured a lot and had little to lose. He had so little to lose that he'd had to learn to set traps with his elbows.

Artie was a natural to complete the threesome. He seethed with rage toward the Rhino. We met after school to formulate the plot. I chaired the meeting and opened the floor to suggestions. Artie voted that we shoot her, but I vetoed. I figured that'd only make her mad.

Timmy mentioned that he'd had some good luck trapping lately and had a whole raft of muskrat carcasses that he didn't know what to do with. What Artie suggested we do with them involved the Rhino and was not only journalistically indescribable, we also figured it was anatomically impossible.

But, the carcasses had possibilities.

Timmy brought some of the muskrat carcasses over to my house and we met for our second round of talks in The Plantation House. I named it "The Plantation House" after seeing pictures of those fine quail-shooting estates in the South. The rest of the family called it "the garage."

Anyway, we got down to business. We knew that Sister Ann Theresa was due for a visit. Sister Ann was The Rhino's Mother Superior. She was a gem: kindly, friendly, and she really liked kids — typical of the kind of teacher they yank out of classroom and make into an administrator.

Anyhow, The Rhino always put The Ruler into retirement during Sister Ann's inspection tours, the only time we got a breather and could act like, well, kids. In our young way, we had already deduced that The Rhino knew that finger-flog-ging was a no-no and hoped to cover it up. We decided to use the occasion of Sister Ann's visit for the coup.

The visit wasn't long in coming. The Rhino had us clean-ing and shining our classroom for two days; we figured that Ann would steam into view about Wednesday of that week. Back at The Plantation House, Timmy cut up several musk-rats, and I tore an old sheet into strips. The logistics were working out, but it was going to take nerve.

When Ann arrived, she visited The Rhino first. We could sense the coolness between the two, and Ann asked a few pointed questions of several of us, but we didn't dare tell the truth. In those days you didn't get to be eleven by being stupid.

Well, Ann moved on to another classroom, and The Rhino let out a visible sigh of relief. At my signal, Timmy, Artie, and I all—so help me—swallowed hard, stuck our tongues out at The Rhino, and flashed her a hand signal indicating the answer to the math problem "Three-take-away-two." The Rhino had The Ruler out of hiding faster than Randolph Scott slapping leather. She was enraged. When the enemy's enraged, she doesn't think clearly.

Ordered front, we took our licks. We shrieked in pain— also in unison—and The Rhino looked shocked. We weren't *supposed* to scream; we weren't *supposed* to be so loud; we weren't *supposed* to do that when the boss was in the build-ing—next door, in fact.

We headed for our seats just as Sister Ann ran into the room to see what was up. Meanwhile, we conspirators took the legs of the dismembered muskrats and held them be-tween our knuckles, the stubs protruding from the sleeves of our shirts. We wrapped our hands and wrists with the cloth strips and waited for Vesuvius to blow.

It didn't take long. Sister Ann asked the three of us to step into the hall. We did. She blanched when she saw our wrapped-up paws, and she asked us to unwrap them. Ac-cording to plan, we gingerly unwrapped the tips of the muskrat legs, red, runny, with bone splinters still showing.

We even had a few ligaments dangling for effect. Sister Ann turned sort of green around the gills and rocked back on her heels.

Phase two: We threw ourselves on the floor, clutching Ann's legs and habit with our stubs, begging her not to say anything to The Rhino—we feared retribution; we *always* got better, we cried, we *always* did. *All* us kids were great healers!

Ann was unmoved; she stormed into the classroom, and we heard a muffled but animated exchange between the two nuns. Throwing out the muskrat legs, we rewrapped our hands and waited. Soon, The Rhino, with Ann behind her, hot-footed it out of the room toward the principal's office. Unnoticed at first, we leaned against the wall. We somehow sensed that this was our last view of the Rhino, and so did she, for she looked back at us as she walked away, glaring. We gave her the unspoken answer to her unspoken question, "What is the square root of 1?"

The next day, we reclined in our seats, shooting paper wads and waiting for the new teacher. In she came.

"I'm Sister Mary," she said, "and I'm here to replace Sister Angela. And if you think things were tough before . . ." She looked straight at me. She didn't finish the rest of the sentence. She didn't have to.

Book Review: The Roadhunter's Guidebook

Not too long ago, a review copy of a new book came over my desk from a little-known but financially unsuccessful publisher.

"The Roadhunter's Guidebook," by Bill Bob Zud, author of "Fixin' yer Mutt: A Paleolitic Guide to Dog Training." This book has to rank as one of the finest pieces of literature for the man who takes his grouse shooting "with ease"; it points out all the fallacies of the so-called "sporting ethic" in a hard-hitting style that followers of Zud have come to know so well.

For example, his chapter on guns and loads has to be considered the state of the art for devotees of roadhunting. Zud recommends, ". . . a good, tight, full-choke in .410. This puts the load into the head and neck of a sitting grouse without damaging any meat, and the low recoil of this gauge

makes it easier to use one-handed out the window. The rela-
tively quiet report of the gun is also less likely to disturb birds
or game wardens that may be around the next bend."

The chapter on hunting vehicles is pure genius as well.
Zud examines the various types available and how they can
help increase the game bag tally. He personally opts for a
new model with a sunroof. While he drives, a partner can
stand up with his upper torso out the sunroof and take the
birds while the car is still moving, adding a bit of zest to this
already-exciting sport. A quiet muffler is a must, he notes.

To those would-be "sportsmen," those that actually get
off the road and walk through the brush with dogs to hunt
these birds, Zud offers some harsh words:

"I think these effeminate snobs are finally being exposed
for what they are—the most effete of the shooting class. Their
insistence on shooting grouse that are flying borders on the
insane. Furthermore, the money they spend on expensive,
snobbish doubles and blooded dogs would buy a first-rate
freezer to hold the birds they *could* kill using my methods. To
show you the difference, a fellow I know—one of this type—
hunted nearly every day of last season and shot only eigh-
teen grouse. I hunted the roads to and from work twice a
week and shot one hundred and twenty-six. Now, I ask you:
who is the *real* grouse hunter?"

The book features a rollicking humor chapter, telling
some of the hilarious antics that Zud and his cronies have
pulled off. For example, he tells how he had to do some really
fast talking to his wife and boss to explain how he spent
thirty days in jail for game-law violations. And, even this
chapter is full of good advice. He notes the best ways to: talk
your way around a game officer, bribe a back-country judge,
and shoot one-handed while not spilling the beer you've got
in the other.

The last chapter is a poignant look to the future. Zud
outlines in detail the best ways to start a son or daughter in a
sport which will stay with them "for life" if they are introduced properly.

"One of the best ways is to make sure that the kid gets to

kill birds. That is why, in the final analysis, we are all out there. If you can get 'em into birds early and they can take ten or twelve the first hunt, then they're hooked for life."

Zud suggests that these youngsters be given plenty of practice handling firearms before the first hunt, recommending, "a beer can on a fence post, a power-line insulator, or the 'o' in a stop sign" as good practice targets. He adds proudly that some of the youngsters he has trained have even moved on to jacklighting deer.

For preseason practice, Zud suggests timing maneuvers, such as quickly bailing in and out of cars and running fifteen feet to pick up a grouse (he uses a retrieving dummy). This adds quickness to the roadhunter's moves, enabling him to cover more ground.

In all, this book will become and remain popular throughout grouse range. Wherever there are birds, there will be those who will want to read it and hunt this way.

Bon Apetit!

Hiya

They were a couple of West Virginians. The twang was evident even from the "hiya" they each gave me as I introduced myself that frosty morning near a grouse cover we had both — they and me — decided to hunt.

We had pulled our cars off the road opposite each other at the choice hillside spot, and after an awkward silence as we eyed one another, they got out of their car and walked across the gravel toward me.

I rolled down the window and we exchanged our "hiya's" and talked in generalities about the day. Finally, noting my Midwestern accent — or maybe the lack of any accent at all — Bob, the smaller of the two, asked if I was a native or hunting there from out of state.

I replied that I was from Pennsylvania by way of Michigan and that I was, indeed, from out of state but had driven down this Wednesday morning to sample the early-winter grouse hunting.

Bill, the other of the pair, mentioned that they always did their hunting, at least they started out, in this large cover. He asked if I'd like to join them.

I'm always a little hesitant about hunting with strangers, so I refused quickly, mentioning that I felt the cover was really theirs and I'd just move on.

Bob said that there was no reason to do that, but didn't push it because I think he sensed my hesitation. Instead, he started talking about hunting, and how great it was to get away for a few hours from his job and to be outdoors for a while. Bill nodded in agreement.

"Tell me, Bill," I asked, "don't you look on hunting as a cruel sport? I mean, it seems hunters are depicted as cruel, ruthless, sub-human people who delight in the torture and death of God's innocent creatures." I wanted to see if they were true hunters, and this is my pet method.

"Well," he began, "I don't rightly see it that way. Bob and I get out about once a week together during the middle of the week. Sure, we could go out with cameras instead of guns, but that's not the way we want it. I think I hunt because man has always hunted, and I think that I'll always hunt. I don't see anything cruel in taking game fairly."

Bob chimed in. "You know, it seems to me that the people who are so all-fired willing to low rate hunters as below human should take a good look at their own lives. Do they like and indeed love most animals more than they do most people? Do they watch TV and shed a tear for the pet dog that gets killed, even in play-acting, and not bat an eye at the evening news that tells of human suffering? If they do, then they have somewhere lost touch with the reality of the human experience, with the need that humans have for other humans. The affection and understanding they feel for animals may have been misdirected away from other people.

"I don't mean to say that a man can't love a dog. But, he's got to remember that it's a dog, not a person. No animal on earth is worth one human, regardless of what the anti's may tell you."

I commented that it was good to hear such a different viewpoint, and we passed some more small talk. I decided to accept their invitation to hunt, and stepped from the car, slipped on my vest, and uncased my Ithaca.

"By the way," I asked as we headed into the roadside brush, "do you fellas always hunt during the week?"

"Yeah, we do," grinned Bill. "Both of us work weekends."

"What do you do?" I asked, hoping I wouldn't sound nosey.

"Bob's a Methodist minister and I'm a Catholic priest. Bob, do you want the right or the left? Let's give Steve the middle. He can't get turned around in the brush that way."

Back Of Beyond

T he old Ford station wagon squeaked to a stop just off the dirt road at the bottom of the long hill. The old man got out and looked back up the hill, marveling that the brakes had held again.

The October sun was starting to dry the frost from the bracken ferns as he let Skip out of her kennel in the back of the car. The Setter, like him, had seen many autumns, many grouse and woodcock. This hunt was going to be just one more in a never-ending string of hunts.

He assembled his old Ithaca, the 20 double's worn barrels glinting in the sun as he clicked the forearm into place. His hands thumbed the lever, and the empty chambers stared up at him like unseeing eyes. Dropping a pair of yellow shells in the chambers, he left the gun open as he swung his leg across the fence that bordered the old railroad grade that skirted the bottom of the hill and headed west, out of sight. It headed for Back of Beyond.

The town by that name had been young when the old man was young. He hadn't known it though, because he'd grown up in another part of the state. It was only after the War that he had moved here and had started poring over old maps to locate grouse cover. It was then that he discovered the name on an old plat map and decided to visit there. He was glad that he had.

Back Of Beyond had been a railroad stopover years ago. It had started as a coal and water stop for the great trains that hauled the great trees to the mills during the late 1880's. As the trees disappeared and the soil was opened to sunlight, the farmers and their plows moved in and the town started to grow. Then farm prices dropped and the young people decided there was more money in the cities. The old folks died off or moved away, and the forest came back, and with it came the grouse and woodcock, and with them came the old man.

When he first came to Back Of Beyond, it was easy to find, not grown over like now. Just follow the old grade west until you came to the first of the old buildings that marked the town square. The shells of a few stores and some pitiful old houses, many collapsed by weather and years, were about all that was left now.

He hunted on the edge of town. One of his favorite spots was right around the old town cemetery. The weathered stones showed the old man what had happened during those early, spare years. The dates and ages on the stones told him there must have been an epidemic of some kind, maybe the flu, that had killed a number of children. The figures told the story: "Josie Ann, beloved daughter, dead at age seven in the year of Our Lord eighteen-hundred and ninety-six, April 6."

And so on.

The other stones told of lives lived and snuffed out early by accident, childbirth, and the rigors of fighting the wilderness every day of a short life. Very few stones showed that the owner had lived past fifty. The old man could remember turning fifty, a long time ago.

He remembered another graveyard near the city. The one where he'd buried Evelyn. He buried her right there next to Jeff. Jeff, with his military headstone and flag and his Silver Star.

Jeff had loved Back Of Beyond too, although his youth made it hard for him to sit still while the old man filled his pipe. Jeff had come to Ev and him late in life, and he never could quite keep up with the boy. Always going, he'd gone away to college and then to the Air Force, and then halfway round the world to a place called Da Nang . . . and finally he'd come home, to the graveyard next to his mother.

But the old man never thought of them as being there. He thought of them as being here, in the Back Of Beyond cemetery.

The old man thought of the dogs who had come here with him for their last hunt, not that they'd known. They'd died, all three of them, in his arms at the vet's office and he'd put them in the car and driven to the old grade and walked back to the town and to the cemetery and he'd buried them under the remnants of the white pines. They'd loved this place the most, and so he'd brought them here.

He had been leaning against a pine as the memories of the place washed over him. A good wife, a good son, good dogs. All gone. For a time, he was like dead too, only still breathing. But slowly, he came to the realization that the worst thing that could happen to a man had already happened to him, and that what years he had left would be spent in fooling with puppies and polishing his Ithaca and hunting grouse. Always, there were grouse. He'd lived for them, and here, here in Back Of Beyond, it was as though the birds lived for him to take his mind from his grief.

He clicked his tongue to Skip. She'd been standing nearby, watching him. He turned his back on the graveyard and headed for a clump of aspen that skirted the old grade and was taking it over in spots.

Skip knew the game, knew the birds. She was old, but

she was determined, and within fifteen minutes, she had a point. The old man's heart was pounding just like it was the first time Robin had pointed a grouse for Jeff—his first. The boy had taken the bird with one swift shot, and the old man had it mounted. It's still in his room back in the city, right where it was the day the boy had left for Vietnam. Everything was the same, even the necktie carelessly thrown over the mirror on his dresser. He had joked to his mother that he'd put it away when he came home, and Ev hadn't ever let anyone touch anything in Jeff's room.

But Jeff had come home in a government-issue casket, and the tie was still there, and the grouse was still staring out the window in his room, and six months later, he'd buried Ev. Like some of the mothers of Back Of Beyond, she hadn't been able to cope with life without her only child. Her heart went, and with it went the last of the joy from the old man's.

But Skip was waiting, and the old man moved in to flush. The bird hammered up through the aspen whips. Even as he triggered the shot, his mind told him "young hen," and after the retrieve, the tailfeathers proved him right. He pocketed the bird. Funny, there wasn't the old feeling. The point had been flawless, the bird courageous, the shot true. But like players who know their parts a bit too well, the thrill was gone.

The parts hadn't changed, it was him. The visit to the doctor hadn't helped. Not by a long shot.

After Ev had died, he knew the worst pages of his life had already been turned, but that was before the visit. His stomach had been giving him fits, so he went. Hadn't been to the doctor since the War, but he went now.

Cancer.

My God, what a horrible word that is.

Cancer.

He had it, and it was going to kill him, and it was going to do it within a year if he was lucky.

If he weren't lucky, it would take two years.

He spurned the surgery which the doctor said probably wouldn't help, and the chemotherapy which would make his hair fall out and, as the old man had told the doctor, "leave an ugly corpse."

Nope, he decided the way to go was to take it like a man. To wait for it. And all the time he'd pray that it would come and get him quickly. He just had Skip now, and some days it was nip and tuck as to who was going to go first. But, October had come, and the bounce came back in her step and she was ready at the door for the opener. Ready to go to Back Of Beyond.

She was all he had. Sometimes the weakness he felt, the pain and the exhaustion, were all he could stand. He'd put dogs down who'd suffered less pain, and one night—one horrible, black night—he'd taken the Ithaca down from the rack and dropped a single shell into the right barrel and raised the muzzle toward his head . . .

But his fighter's heart said no, not this way. Not now. Better to wait for it. No sense helping The Bastard. Death.

Skip had another point, and a woodcock twittered up. The Ithaca was true again, and the retrieve was perfect. The little weight it added in his gamebag seemed greater than he knew it to be. He loved woodcock, loved them for their mysterious ways and their nighttime comings and goings. Years ago, he and Ev and Jeff had spent spring nights listening to the 'cock sing. They'd watch until full dark and then walk back to the car, hand-in-hand and eat a sandwich as the stars came out.

Years ago.

Three lifetimes ago.

Now, they were gone, and The Bastard was winning.

He sat down on the old stone fence where he always sat at noon to eat lunch, only today, there was no lunch. The pain and the nausea made eating a cruel joke these days. Lucky he could even shuffle along today; eating was out of the question. But he fed the sandwich he carried out of habit to Skip, and she begged for more.

Finally, he decided to head for the grade and the car and home. Skip followed slowly, as if knowing that this was the last time, the last visit to Back Of Beyond.

They stopped by the cemetery once more as they passed by the old town, and the old man leaned, and then sat down, under a huge flaming sugar maple, the leaves falling into breathless air against a sky as blue as Ev's eyes had once been. And Jeff's.

He sat there, and Skip lay down next to him, and the old man's mind wandered. To Jeff, to Ev, to other dogs, to the birds. He relaxed. Funny, he hadn't really relaxed like this in years. Maybe never.

As his mind journeyed, the leaves fell on him and Skip, and the sun slipped lower in the sky.

And finally, the leaves nearly covered them both. Skip stood, shook, prodded the old man with her nose, licked his face, and turned toward the old grade and the car.

But the old man didn't follow. Not this time. He was already home.

To Shoot A Quail

1 0:02 A.M. A picturesque field of lespedeza south of the
Mason-Dixon line. The dog is a banjo-ribbed pointer,
liver and white with ticking through the white. A big
male we'd call "rawboned" if it weren't so trite, he is a good
covey dog and a passable singles dog. You have been invited
down to shoot quail by a business associate, one whose
friendship is important to your company and your own
future. But after arriving, you find that he is a likeable South-
erner who, despite his wealth, has struck up with you, a
Yankee working stiff, a friendship based on guns and dogs
and birds.

You are hunting on his plantation, a family plot of several
thousand acres which his unreconstructed grandparents
managed to wrest back from the carpetbaggers after the War

Between the States—you have decided to call it that or The War for Southern Independence if the subject somehow comes up.

You have brought along your grouse gun and found, to your relief, that it matches within acceptable parameters the southern quail—"bird"—gun. Your host is shooting a 16-gauge double; your 20 side-by-side is not viewed as foreign in his gentle company.

The dog has frozen rigidly on point where the lespedeza—a word which you have not yet got up the courage to try aloud—bunches thickly around some rotting timbers, remnants of a sharecropper's garden fence. In the background is the shack those unfortunates lived in until they figured out that there was no way they would ever be out of debt, so they fled in the night, headed north for the growing auto plants of Detroit or the steel mills of Pittsburgh to merge their blood with the other immigrants from our own nation and elsewhere.

Your host's dog handler, Jacob, an unlit cigar clenched in his teeth, is crooning to the dog, low and soothingly, telling the animal he is the finest piece of horseflesh he's ever seen. With one hand on his flushing whip, Jacob uses his free hand to wave the two of you into position. Now, it begins.

It is at least twenty-five yards from where you and your host stand to the dog, and another fifteen yards to where you figure the quail are bunched in a tight knot. You make the first strides forward, keeping pace with your host who is not tarrying. Hmmmm. Must be important to get to the point quickly, but without hurrying, like when your dog has a grouse nailed back in New Hampshire. You wonder, absently, why Jacob calls the dog, "Ticker," a fine piece of horseflesh. Why not "dogflesh?" Why not just a "good dog?"

The breeze coming toward you carries a hint of bayou water, a warm breeze. You wonder if the kids are shoveling snow back home like they said they would. Sure they are, you paid them in advance, didn't you? Would they take the money and not do the job? Sure. Rotten kids.

The dog is now fifteen yards from you and closing. A

patch of some kind of thorny bush brushes against your pant leg, and you immediately think: "Snake." You can feel your eyes widen and you look down quickly. Damn snakes. Why did Jacob and your host plan your shooting morning around when the snakes would be out—about mid-morning. Ever since you were six and your older brother shoved a garter snake into your sleeping bag, you've hated snakes. You never see snakes hunting in New Hampshire. Here, you have to watch where you put every foot.

Five yards from the dog, now. What happens if the covey cuts toward the old sharecropper's cabin, is it a social error to shoot toward a building, even if it's empty and unused? Sure wish you'd asked.

And what happens if the dog chases the covey? Do you shoot and maybe endanger the dog? No, of course not. But what if the dog is unsteady to wing—do you shoot and imprint a bad habit on another man's dog or do you wait to see what happens? That's it, if the dog breaks, you'll wait until your host shoots and then *you'll* shoot. But, what if the covey cuts your way and you're the only one with a shot? Better watch the damn dog—sure hope he's broke. Back home, Ruthie wouldn't break, not on a grouse or a woodcock, or all the quail in the state of Alabama. Would have brought her, too, if it hadn't been for the damn snakes. Snakes'll kill a grown Yankee setter that's never seen one before. Besides, airline stiffs would have lost her. Yep, you'd be walking in on this dog's point while Ruthie was sitting in a baggage cart on Guam.

You're even with the dog, now. Ticker walleyes you as you pass by. You like that. You like a dog that needs the men with the guns. Ruthie walleyes, too. When a dog does that, he's telling you he sees you and he's glad you're there and he wants you to do well, and he'll wait here while you go do what it is you've come to do. Funny, two steps ago, Ticker was another slabsided pointer. His rolling eyes have made him a friend.

Well, Ticker's going to stay put, so that takes care of the problem of shooting if he breaks. Now remains the problem of shooting. Okay, all the books you read told you what to do: Pick out a bird—one bird—in the covey and focus only on that bird. Never mind the rest. Stay with that bird and shoot him. If you miss, shoot at him again. If you hit, try for another, nearby bird. Don't swing across your host's line of fire, and take your time. The books all said that quail really aren't moving that fast—they just sound that way.

But they used to tell you that about grouse, too, only they lied—grouse really *are* moving that fast. Maybe your reflexes are as slow as you've always suspected, and what's slow to someone else is fast to you. If one quail is fast, are twelve quail as fast as one quail to the twelfth power?

Okay, okay, alright, alright. Take a breath, now, dummy. You're almost there. You know your gun, the birds are in the open, and you're shooting from the open toward cover—Jacob saw to that. He knows that the birds will fly to cover and you can get straight-away shots this way—you remember that from reading Havilah Babcock. Babcock knew a lot about quail shooting, yessir. He said all you have to do is watch the bird and then point at it and shoot—nothing to it. Really. The thumping in your ears is getting loud, the old adrenalin rush, the salty taste of sweat on your upper lip.

You know, business in this decade is tough. Do you shoot the best you can and maybe outshoot your host? That might be bad for business, maybe even bad form socially. But if you laid off a bit, your host might figure you're trying to patronize him and *that* would be bad, too—he wouldn't want to get himself tied up with someone who didn't always do his best, right? Besides, at home, you never *let* anyone win at anything. You wouldn't even let the kids win at checkers when they were little. Hope the kids are shoveling the snow. Rotten kids.

Then, they are up. God, there must be two dozen of them! Some of them have white faces, some sort of buff-colored. You know that the white-faced ones are the little cockbirds, the others are the hens. They come up with a roar—that's it, a *roar*. It isn't like the thunder of grouse, nowhere near the twitter of a woodcock—it sounds like a bunch of bees right up close. You can feel yourself go bug-eyed, like you always do when birds are up—you don't blink until it's over. Once, up home, you got a twig in the eye because of that habit, trying to shoot a grouse all bug-eyed like that. Started wearing shooting glasses right after that. Didn't wear any today, though. They don't seem right down here.

Your gun moves like it's full of cement. Your muscles are screaming at you, "For Godssake get moving—they'll be a mile off and you won't get a shot. Hurry—HURRY!!"

The gun is at your face, now, your left hand cradles the barrels and you feel your right elbow come up high—way high in that peculiar shooting style you have that has given stockfitters the twitches. A bird bores away and you hold on him, but he's crossing, now, crossing toward your host's side, so you pull off and find another. There! A sassy little cock.

You can hear your host's 16 go off and a bird cartwheels down. You see it peripherally. You haven't shot yet. If that first bird hadn't crossed to his side, you'd have beat him. It's important that you shoot first. You're a grouse hunter. You're all quick. Damn, those birds are moving!

SPAT! The 20 laces a load of eights at the little cock. He tumbles and drops. Only drops about four feet and he's in the grass. These birds don't get high. You'd be willing to bet that a good quail gun is stocked lower than a woodcock gun. A woodcock gun should be stocked high to keep the rising birds right on the end of the barrel. Don't have to cover 'em to hit 'em, just follow 'em to the top of their spin and *pow*!

POW! The left barrel catches a cutter that had almost made the brush. Your host must have shot at the same time, because you are aware of another bird dropping, this one on his side. Well, slow on the first bird, but quick on the second. Maybe there is something to this more-time-than-you-think business.

Jacob is hollering, now. "Dead bird! Dead Bird!" Ticker is cruising past you, and soon all four of the quail are in hand to be admired, then into Jacob's sack they go. Your host is complimenting you, and you are reliving your shots, both of you, the way hunters do, explaining so that you can understand yourself what happened. The explanations are for you, not for the other man.

As you turn to leave, your host claps you on the shoulder and says, "Nice shooting. Looks like a Yankee grouse hunter can take to bird shooting real fine. If you do business like you shoot, we won't have any problems."

You have that glow going, now, the flow that tells you that you've done something very well. You look at your watch — 10:03. Only a minute's passed — only a lifetime.

As you cross the field, watching Ticker racing, looking for another covey, your host mentions, "By the way, I've got to admire your nerve. Never saw anyone step right over a snake like that without at least flinchin' a *little* bit."

If Only

"Tell me, Mr. Smith, will you be taking your shooting on extended periods this autumn, or are business considerations going to keep you inside during the days to come?"

My firearms man, Jenkins, always asks me this well in advance of the season; it gives him time to prepare my shotguns and ammunition so that I have just the right gun/load combinations. But, I always have to tell him my plans so that he can get things just so.

"Well, Jenkins," I meditated, "let's see. My assistant JW has things in hand, so I'll be leaving for an extended woodcock shoot into the Provinces in mid-September. Native birds, you know, so I'll want my light 20 gauge with number ten shot in the right barrel, backed with nine's in the left barrel, I should think."

"Will you be shooting over your setter, Buck?" he asked.

"Yes, why do you ask?"

"Well, because Buck normally holds his birds less tight than, say Jess or one of your other dogs. I'd suggest that you also take along your 12 bore light game gun, the one with the 27½-inch barrels. In the event that leaf fall comes early during your stay or the birds are not holding sufficiently well for Buck due to dry conditions, you may be happy that you have it along. That gun is bored improved cylinder and choke. It weighs but five pounds, ten ounces, so the weight is negligible. I'll send off straightaway for some British game loads in size eight shot, 2½-inch cartridge cases. It would be good to have a spare gun along anyway, Sir."

"Good thinking, Jenkins," I replied.

"After woodcock, what?" Jenkins was busy scribbling notes.

"I think I'll take the train west to the Prairies and go for some sharptails and prairie chickens."

"Hmmmmm," Jenkins puzzled, and mumbled to himself: "Size six shot in the heavily proofed Purdey should suffice. I'll back that gun with the Churchill with the twenty-five-inch barrels and high rib. Two cases of cartridges should do it."

"Then," I continued, "perhaps I'll head for the Eastern Shore for some waterfowling. Nothing fancy here, Jenkins, this is sort of down-home country, if you know what I mean. That should take me until the Christmas Holidays, at which point I'll be home for a bit."

"If 'nothing fancy' is the watchword here, sir, I'd suggest that you take your pair of Parkers in 12 bore. They're both built on the #2 frame, and in the VHE grade, they're not too ostentacious for the people you're likely to be shooting with. Are any of these men like that Mr. Lichon that stopped by here the other day with that—uh—*repeating* shotgun?"

"Yes, Jenkins, I'm afraid that many of them are. The Parkers will do just fine."

"After the Holidays, will it be south for quail on The Plantation?"

"I suppose, Jenkins. By the way, for the waterfowling, are you sending copper four's again this year? Those worked well."

"Yes sir. About the Plantation. I was in communication with Daniel, your overseer, and he told me that the birds— 'partridges,' he calls them—are up in number again. Naturally, you'll want the 16 Parker."

"Naturally."

"And then, I would suppose it's on to Denmark for the duck shooting again this year, am I right, sir?"

"Quite right, Jenkins."

"Am I to assume that Africa is out of the question for this year? Especially with the turmoil they are having over there geopolitically."

"No, Jenkins, I think I'll pop over for a spot of buff shooting and maybe a rogue elephant or two. I've heard the jumbo are getting a bit uppity and I'd like to help sort some of the blighters out, as they say over there."

Jenkins was furiously making notes about what express rifles he would pack and where he could get some .404 solids.

"One last question, sir, and then I'll be off."

"Certainly, Jenkins, what is it?"

"Sir, do you think it likely that perhaps *this* is the year?"

"You mean the year I actually learn to hit birds, Jenkins?"

"Yes, sir."

"Perhaps, Jenkins, perhaps."

The Gun Cabinet Shuffle

I was at the gun club the other day, sort of trying to look invisible because they were about to post my score on the board, when in walks my pal, Roadkill. Roadkill looks like he stopped off at the blood bank to make a donation and got overly generous. Even under his fingernails, he's white.

I say to Roadkill—Roadkill gets his name from being cook at our grouse camp where some of his recipes for the annual Game Dinner are a little suspect—anyway, I say to Roadkill: "Wattinell happened to you? Did somebody run over your setter?"

Roadkill looks at me sort of blank and shakes his head. "Almost as bad. You know those three doubles I bought, the ones in mint condition new in the box? The ones I had hidden in the crawlspace under my house so my wife wouldn't find them and sell 'em? Well, she decided to hose down the garage and she sprayed 'em with water—about a week ago. I looked under there today and they're sitting in a sea of rust."

This got me thinking, right after I wiped the tears from my eyes, of the lengths that some guys go to hide the number of guns they actually own.

The oldest ploy in the world is the old I bought-a-new-one-with-the-money-I-got-from-selling-an-old-one number. Most wives will fall for this, provided you have a safe place to hide all of those that should have been sold but weren't. This ruse seems to work well because in our early days of collecting, most of us *had* to sell an old one to finance a new one. Then came the day when we vowed to never let one go because we always wished we had it back later anyhow.

I have a friend who's a great one for pulling off the "gun cabinet shuffle." Since he's never satisfied with the way a gun looks/feels/fits/shoots, he's always trundling one or more off to the gunsmith for some type of work. This makes for easy pickups because the cast of characters in his cabinet is constantly changing—his really good stuff is in storage in a place he won't tell me about.

One rule that most of the guilty try to use is to never—but never—allow the wives together in one room, not even for funerals. If they are together any longer than forty-five seconds, they start comparing notes, like: "How is that gun that my Bill was fixing for your Tom?" This, of course, uncovers that other standard gambit whereby you pretend that a new gun of yours is an old one owned by another guy and you're doing something to the stock for him. At times like this, you feel, all things taken into account, that you'd really rather be in Philly.

Roadkill and I took the wives to an RGS banquet last August—the first time the two women had ever laid eyes on each other. All the way down in the car, Road and I keep up a litany about politics, the weather, who our favorite newscaster is, why our friend Harvey can't hit grouse or really any other target that's moving . . . you name it, we talked about it. I mean, when I'm not talking, Roadkill is.

Finally, the inevitable happened. We both stopped talking to catch a breath at the same time. At that precise instant, Roadkill's wife turns to mine and says, "So, how many guns does your Steve say that my Tom has?" Even though it's August, Roadkill reaches over and turns on the heater.

The other big problem is when a casual acquaintance stops by, a guy you've met at the gun club and bragged about your gun collection to. On an evening when you figure everything's going to go okay, this guy stops by. Since you don't recognize his car in the driveway, you don't even bother to go to the door, you just sort of snap your fingers at the Storm-and-Strife and she trots over to answer the bell. You're only half listening as you hear the visitor tell your wife: "Hello, I'm a friend of _____ and I stopped by to take a look at the 16 gauge Parker he just bought." The wife appears and in even, measured, deliberate tones, says, "It's for you." Ever noticed how sometimes they can make it snow inside?

The day after that dinner I was talking about, Roadkill calls me to tell me that his wife had left him an itemized bill of what he spent in the last year on guns, dogs, books, prints, Jack Daniels, and other related frivolities. Her note ends up ". . . no, Tom, don't think of this money as wasted or even begrudged; think of it as a microwave, a new couch, new tires on my car, doctor bills . . . "

Looking Good

If you made me stick my hand on a Bible and swear to it, I'd have to look you right in the eye and tell you that the well-dressed upland hunter of the 1980's doesn't really do much for me.

It seems like the more time I spend in the coverts, the more I see the glad rags come out of the closet and onto the hunters. If you spend any time at all around the guilty themselves, and we all do, you're likely to hear more talk of fabric, color, texture, and durability (not to mention the well-tailored fit) than you do of chokes, gauges, barrel lengths, and who went 0 for 15 on the old Thompson Place last week. The whole thing sounds vaguely like a Liberace family reunion.

On most days, when I go hunting, I'm afraid that I'd have to plead guilty to not having my brush pants match my shooting jacket, and neither of these is color-coordinated with my shirt.

I know, I know. I'm ashamed of it, but what can I do? While I'm at it, I may as well admit that my boots no longer have the high luster they once had two hundred rough-country miles ago, and the left boot's lace has a knot in it. Sad.

I once hunted with a fellow who chuckled at the "shabby" clothing he saw on another hunter during breakfast at a diner. I looked at the object of his ridicule and noticed the guy wasn't color-coordinated either, but I felt superior because *both* of his bootlaces had knots.

Three hours later, over a nice point, my well-dressed companion nearly shot my head off trying to steal a bird from me.

Beauty is only skin deep, but arrogance is to the bone.

A Nice Place

L ast fall, I went back to one of my favorite places, a stump that sits above a gin-clear brook that scrambles over a beaver dam in the middle of a pretty good woodcock covert.

When I go there, it's usually alone—just my dog and me. I always pack a lunch and end up at my stump at noon.

This past year, the sun was right, the sky blue, I had two birds with two shots, and I was sharing pieces of my lunch with Jess when she'd paddle back to the streambank from a little swim. I was thinking how lovely this place was and how lucky I was to have such a good dog and a good place to hunt.

Then I started thinking about if my life ended right then and there, I couldn't think of too many things I'd be leaving undone. I thought that maybe somebody could see that I could stay right there for Eternity listening to the stream and counting the leaves as they floated by.

And then, I wondered how many people had made the awful mistake of thinking those things and then had gone and done something about those thoughts, and I sure wasn't like that, was I? But my Parker, my sweet, smooth, deadly old Parker, was right there, and it *was* such a nice day and all . . .

I can't be sure, but I don't think I'll go back to that place again.

From There To Here

I started life as a chunk or two of steel and some European walnut in the year of our Lord nineteen-hundred and thirty. It was, I remember, in September of that year that a Frenchman came to the small, eight-man gunmaker's outside of St. Etienne, France.

Across the horizon, but not yet visible to the population, the winds of war were stirring. Hitler was ruminating about the horrible terms of the Treaty of Versailles, and the Great Depression had thrown the globe into such an economic upheaval that only the demands of a Great War could put it right again.

But to the slightly built Frenchman who visited with the head of the gunmaker's firm, all of this was far off. He, well mannered and impeccably tailored, comes from what you

Americans call "old money" and his greatest concern right now was getting fitted for a game gun for the shooting of driven birds on his estate.

The measurements are taken, minutiae discussed, a deposit of a goodly number of francs changes hands, and he is gone.

My barrels and action are cut and meticulously hand-fitted. The walnut is cut and carved and shaped and inletted, and the engraving is done on my boxlock action. The Frenchman would have preferred a sidelock, but the size of his hand dictated that a boxlock, with its stronger wood, be made.

The Frenchman comes back, periodically, to chat and inspect work-in-progress. When my barrels and action are in the white stage, the final fitting and patterning is done. Almost two years to the day, in 1932, I am delivered.

My French owner and I spend several seasons shooting driven pheasants. I am a 12-bore, five pounds, ten ounces with 27½-inch barrels, straight grip, splinter forend, double triggers. In the Frenchman's hands, I am quite deadly.

The years pass, and the French government grows worried over the German juggernaut which has rolled over Czechoslovakia and Poland. Daily, the Luftwaffe grows more bold. Taxes are raised to strengthen the military, and the rich Frenchman finds there is no money left to pay his gamekeeper and maintain his estate. I am placed in the gun cabinet in his study to await pleasanter days.

In 1939, my owner is called back to service. He is a major in the French reserve. He wipes me down one more time, swings me, and places me in the cabinet. He leaves to join his regiment on the eastern border. There, he dies in combat. I hear his servants, packing to leave themselves, discuss the fact that their beloved master did not go to a soldier's grave alone. He was found slumped over a .30-caliber machine gun surrounded by seventeen dead German regulars. Remembering how he handled me, I am surprised he did not get them all.

The place is all but deserted, and I hear the sound of battle in the distance. The months pass. The servants, who come now from town to check on the locked estate, tell each other after the June, 1940 surrender, the little gunmaker's shop was visited by German soldiers. The master craftsmen there were taken back to Dussledorf to build aircraft firearms. They will never return. Sporadically over the next several months, I hear gunfire as Partisan fights German. But soon, only silence.

Sometime in the summer of 1944, the shelling grows heavier. The servants have locked me away in the cellar and have not come now for many months. The rust is thick on my barrels, and the dampness worries my wood. I am surprised that the house has not been violated during the occupation.

Then, some soldiers enter the house. They speak a funny language, and they search the house with submachine guns readied. They are, as I find out, American paratroopers. They are painfully young looking, but they have the same old eyes my French owner had when he got his call to war—solemn and brave and resigned.

One of these lads spies me and I become a spoil of war. He says that after the War, my 12-bore barrels will be tracking Iowa pheasants. For now, I am dismantled and placed in his haversack.

The weeks and months pass quickly. My new owner and I are in the thick of almost every fight, but he is a good shot and a clever survivor. He is decorated. The war ends. He is discharged.

His superiors look the other way as we are mustered home and then out of the service.

Sometime in the late fall of 1945, we step off a bus in a place called Winterset, Iowa. Eight days later, my new owner is married, moved back to the farm he inherited from his parents, and I am knocking cold big, gaudy Iowa cockbirds.

For thirty-nine years, I am taken from the rack each fall to do what it is I was built to do. My new owner grows older. His children, once small, grow and marry and move away, and once I can remember that a tornado came and took away part of the house. One fall, my young soldier does not come to the gun cabinet for me. I know, by now, the signs of death.

A son, one who especially liked me, takes me as an inheritance. He is a young accountant in Michigan now, just getting started and with a young family. Dollars are tight, and I am valuable, so he says. He takes me to a gun shop and sells me. It is done quickly and he does not look back as he leaves. Shoes for growing children are needed more than a 12-bore memory.

I sit on the gunsmith's used gun rack for several months. One day, a slightly built man in his 30's happens by. He looks so much like my long dead Frenchman. He spots me. He picks me up tenderly, throws me to his shoulder, and swings me. The drop at comb and heel seem perfect. The cast-off is comfortable to me. He marvels at my trim weight.

He never puts me back down. He strides to the gunsmith, swallows hard, and asks the price. After some bargaining, a deal is struck and I go home with the New Owner.

He carefully disassembles me and oils and inspects all my parts, refinishes my stock, and brings my coin-finished receiver back to gleaming newness. He mutters about how tight my chokes are because he hunts a small bird called "woodcock," while I was built for pheasants. A craftsman not unlike my original builders takes some of the choke from my right barrel.

That next fall, in my newfound vitality, I am carried through unspeakable thickets behind a little orange and white English setter. Suddenly, the dog stops and stiffens. In France, the dogs were all retrievers to be used for picking up birds after a drive; in Iowa, my owner used farm collies to push pheasants into the air. This is new to me.

I can feel my new owner's heart racing against my stock tucked against his ribs. He strides in ahead of the dog, shuffling his feet. A small, long-billed bird twitters up through the thicket. Quick, my barrels are up and tracking the bird. Just as my muzzles pass the bird's head, my front trigger is pulled, and a light load of #8 shot puffs this strange target. The dog fetches and holds the bird while my new owner takes a photograph of me, the dog, and the bird. Then, on we go after another bird.

We shoot two more and then stop by a brook and watch leaves float by. He tells the dog we are under the limit, but that's fine. The day is clear, leaves are every color, and there are quiet brooks and streams. My new owner treats me, his dog, and his birds like friends. Without trying for the last two woodcock to complete his limit, my new owner fills his pipe, puts his dog at heel, and takes me home.

I think I'm going to like it here.

C.SMITH

The Quail Caper

A long about last August, when the preseason crazies started to hit everybody, my pal Roadkill calls up with one of his schemes. We've both got young setters, and Road figures it'd be a good idea if we chipped in fifty bucks or so each, buy a bunch of quail, get the proper permits from the game department, work our dogs on the quail, and get in some early gunning to boot.

Sounds great, says I, let's do it. I designated Roadkill as chief negotiating agent for the Great Quail Caper and thought little more of it. I shoulda.

Road calls me up a couple weeks later to announce that the quail are there. I quickly bum a collapsible pen from a pal and go to pick up my half of the quail (by the way, "a bunch" of quail translates into about ten for fifty clams). I get my five

127

home where I stow them in the garage out of the weather. It turns out that I've also stowed them out of any reasonable form of incarceration because they stay in the cage about like water stays in a sieve. My setter's first ever point was on a quail that got behind the rototiller and wouldn't come out.

The problems started to mount up pretty quick when I checked out the prices of stuff I had to buy to support a family of quail: a call-back pen, a quail harness, feed, grit, and a smelt-dipping net to catch the little beggars when I was done with them after a training session. Each quail could have had a decent education for what I shelled out on him— or her. I never could tell the difference, although I assume that they could.

I'm also pretty certain that my kids could, too. When the time came to shoot the birds over my dog's flawless and salivatingly intense points, I trooped out to the garage to arrange for a few volunteers. The kids trooped along.

Taking the smelt net in hand, I made a swipe at one bird on a rafter. "OH GOD, NO! NOT EDNA!" Hmmmmmm.

Another stab at a bird scuttling behind the fertilizer. "NOT BUFORD, DON'T TAKE BUFORD!" Things weren't looking good for the home team.

By the time I had made a capture attempt at each of my quail, I found out they weren't my quail anymore. In fact, I found out that they weren't quail, even; they were members of the family, each with a real name, a well-defined personality, and with a fan club of three.

So, I guess you've pretty well figured things out. The quail now live in luxury in my garage, doing unspeakable things to the hood of my station wagon. They eat better than maybe half the people of Bolivia.

I haven't heard from Roadkill for a while.

Think I'll stop by and say hi.

How To Lie, Cheat, and Connive for Better Shooting and Enhanced Reputation

One of the toughest things about grouse and woodcock hunting, to those who really understand, is to find covers that are productive, of the right age, offer fairly decent shooting, and are *private*.

Everybody knows that keeping a cover secret is a chore, and jokes about blindfolding people before they are taken into a good one are often cruelly true. There are ways to make sure that a casual acquaintance never returns to a cover with *his* buddies, but they are illegal in every state and province and violate the odd commandment or two.

Naturally, there are ways that covers can be masked, newcomers can be discouraged from interloping, and slightly known shooters from your gun club can be misled. However, the main way to guarantee your private shooting in your private covers—without interference—is to learn how to tell lies.

Not knowing how, exactly, I contacted a few friends who number among their faults the sport of fishing. Everybody knows that the hook-and-line set has taken the science of lying and honed it to an art form, so I figured this was the place to start.

From what they told me, the lies fall into certain categories. First off, there's the kind that has to be told to the wives of the guilty so that they can get to go hunting in the first place. This type of lie usually centers around two or three basic premises. Premise number one is that the bigger the lie, the more believable it is. Instead of telling the little woman you're going hunting, tell her that you are doing field research at the request of the state fish and game department, that only a man of your expertise would do, and you have to be gone every Saturday during the season to help in this important work.

With a little ingenuity, you could produce an official-looking letter on government stationery to back up your claims. A friend of mine, a superintendent of schools, uses this ruse to go fishing. It's been working for years for him.

Another lie involves the use of the hunting buddy to substantiate your claim to hunting freedom. Get the other guy to feign an illness, something terminal but rare. Note that the guy is sensitive about his condition, but the prognosis is lousy. Then, tell the little woman that you are going to do everything in your power to make sure that he gets as much sport as possible before the Grim Reaper makes his call. Naturally, your wife will agree 100% and will insist that you even use the vacation time you've saved to visit Grandmother Fishbait in the summer to go hunting. Have the "illness" linger, and you can parlay this into several season's worth of sport. When the wife gets suspicious, claim a miracle cure and think of something else.

Scientists and anthropologists tell us that the yearnings we experience during the autumn months are genetically remembered feelings of migration that our ancestors had when the herds that fed them started the fall movement to winter pasture. When the herds moved, we moved, and this autumn restlessness is with us yet today, even though we are a "civilized" species, after a fashion.

If the grouse and woodcock hunter has an urge to be up and gone when the sun's rays slant just so, the man's wife usually has an urge to clean up the family cave like her long-ago, long-vanished Neanderthal sister.

To the shooter, this situation is, as my daughter says, "less than cool." In truth, no two people can look at a situation and see it entirely the same. That is why we need diplomats, judges, and referees. Wives definitely don't look at things the way we do: Where a weather forecast of morning fog but clearing in the afternoon gives you and me thoughts of ideal scenting conditions for our dogs, wives think in terms of cleaning the garage.

The hunter, then, must be fast on his feet to keep one step ahead. That is why I will pass along a few excuses that I have used successfully over the years to free myself from the domestic drivel that keeps me from the cover.

One of the best is what I call the "Look-At-All-The-Things-I-Don't-Do" gambit. By pointing out that you don't bowl, play poker, shoot pool in some den of ill repute which serves distilled spirits, or shoot skeet, you can make yourself look put-upon and deserving of just this little pleasure. If you do any or all of the above, point out that you are not a heroin addict, even though it'd probably end up being cheaper in the long run. You now have the tacit agreement of your mate that you are deserving of a few mornings out—say forty or fifty—during season.

Another excuse I've found helpful is the "Stick and Carrot Routine." In this one, the hunter promises to do some long-waiting repair project around the home right after he returns from hunting. Talk glowingly about the placement of that painting Aunt Agatha gave you for Christmas last year, or discuss minutiae about the new shower door you've promised to put up. When you return from hunting, act brave, but let a small limp creep into your walk, and try—unsuccessfully, of course—to hide the pain from that old football injury. Pretty quick, you're off the well-known hook.

The third in this series of excuses might be called the "Team Approach," or more correctly, the "Secret Weapon." This one takes a little timing, but it never fails. At a time in the afternoon that you think is exactly right, just mention that you don't think you'll go woodcock hunting tomorrow because you have a lot do to around the house. Mention that you haven't been home much on the weekends lately—ignoring her retort that "at all" could be substituted for "much." Then, let the subject drop. Wife is either shocked blinkless or in a state of euphoria. Her mind is a blank canvas awaiting your brush strokes. This is how you want her.

At a prearranged time, your grouse and woodcocking pal phones you. You make sure that the whole house hears your end of the conversation. You loudly defend your right to stay home this Saturday. You announce that Mom And The Kiddies are more important to you this weekend, and that you are not wasting another weekend stomping through scratchy cover. The shock threatens to send her over the edge.

Slamming the receiver down, you hotly question why YOU always have to be the one to go hunting with that guy. Is it *your* fault that the other guy's wife won't let him out of the house save this one day? Is it *your* fault that he has no other friends on earth and that he is in a state of suicidal depression from which only *you* can save him? So what if the character *is* the godfather of your firstborn, right is right.

By now, Wife is in tears, and she demands that you phone back—nay, she insists—that you make peace. You resist, asking why a friendship which has lasted since the third grade should have anything to do with hunting? You finally relent, and at Wife's bidding, offer to go hunting as a truce offering between old friends. She is flushed with victory and a feeling of Christian peacemaking; you surrender in abject silence. Excusing yourself to go buy a pouch of tobacco, you stop at the nearest phone booth to repeat the opposite end of the scenario so that your buddy can spring free too.

All of the preceding goes to prove that grouse and woodcock hunters enjoy their sport to the utmost, derive the greatest pleasure from the little things, and have learned to be damned fast on their feet!

The other types of lies the hunter must learn to tell are the kinds involving the hiding of covers from the prying eyes of other shooters. Hiding the car near the cover does no good, neither does sweeping out tire tracks on a dirt road. Masking the direction of the covers works on only the most obtuse, so the old-fashioned fib works best.

In reverse of the usual fisherman's scam, it is best to always maintain that you shoot almost no birds whatsoever. Spend a lot of time griping about the phases of the moon, quizzing the other guy about *his* covers, and suggesting that you may just pack it in and go to New Brunswick, hire a guide, take your shooting there, and to hell with the local stuff.

Naturally, anybody listening to your litany will figure you are really a slouch as a hunter and will cross you off. In addition, some poor slob may even take pity on you and invite you along to one of his covers. You now have added another one to your list (provided you hunt on days you know he doesn't) and you've divulged none of your own.

Another way to hide your woodcock covers is to take a few birds you've shot to the gun club to give them away. Ask the woodcock hunters there to identify the birds for you, give them to him because you hate the taste, and talk glowingly about the prospects of great duck or pheasant shooting.

If keeping the covers secret is a chore, covering up your own ineptitude with a smoothbore is even worse. You are not dealing with strangers here, but with people who know both you and your abilities, so a fresh stock of lies about why you missed are in order before each season begins.

I admire the fellow who can miss both barrels at a going away bird, laugh at himself, and shrug off the experience. I fight waves of nausea with each missed shell, and even if I connect, if the gun was not mounted just so, or I got lucky, I'm concerned. I don't want "lucky." I want "good." Most days I'll take lucky.

Knowing this, how do you mask your misses under a believable barrage of verbiage? Well, to start off with, you have to be willing to admit, about once every two trips, that you really *did* miss for no good reason. Then your excuses will be better accepted when you do use them. It's the old case of crying wolf. Then, as far as excuses go, the best way is to divide these into several categories and go from there, rotating categories as the situation permits.

One category is the faulty equipment bracket. Wearing the wrong type of clothing makes you uncomfortable in a woodcock and grouse cover, so blame the duds for a miss. The coat binds, the pants weren't thick enough to turn the briars, and so on. But, make sure that you do the complaining before you ever get into the cover. If you wait until you miss before making excuses, it'll sound like you're making excuses.

You can fudge on this category a bit too. If you miss a bird, quickly pull out an empty shell that is at least fifteen years old—the old paper kind with the top wad—and blame the ammunition. Make sure your partner does not see you take the real empty from your gun.

Another way is to blame the gun. Once, I missed a wide open grouse with the first barrel at twenty yards—straight away! I was shocked to the point that I didn't even fire the second barrel. Instead, I got busy on my lie. Thinking quickly, I pushed the release lever on the forearm and claimed I hadn't assembled the gun correctly, and when throwing up the piece to shoot, it had come apart. My companion bought it—until someone reads this to him.

Sometimes you can have a miss make you look like an expert. Claim that you missed because the bird was so close you were trying to shoot it with the edge of your pattern, and cuss glowingly. Partner walks away muttering, "Edge of the pattern; I can't hit 'em with the whole damned thing!" You look good, he feels like a chump, which is the way it should be.

Naturally, thick cover is good for excuses aplenty. When you miss one, pick up a piece of deadfall off the ground.

Hold it up so partner can see it, and lie through your teeth about how you just put your whole load into that branch instead of the bird. Partner thinks, now, that you would undoubtedly have scored except for fate and the limb.

Another way is to bring along a pair of badly scratched shooting glasses, even with large gaping cracks. Make a big production of showing these off before you actually start hunting. Say that even though you can hardly see through them, you'll wear them anyway because you value your eyesight. Once in the cover, switch glasses. If you miss, you've got your excuse. If you hit, you can point out what a great shot you are, being able to score even with such crummy optics. Remember to switch back before partner sees you again.

Lastly, try a variation of the War Wound technique. Claiming an old injury, pick the easiest routes through the cover, making partner play dog. This puts you in the best position for a shot, and if you make it, again you look a cut above the average, what with your bad health and all.

Looking for excuses to buy new and expensive goodies for hunting comes a bit harder. New guns can be sneaked in and out, but things like four-wheel-drive vehicles take some thought. Point out that you've had it with your wife having to drive the kids to school through deep snow and you worry about her in that little imported tin can because of the survival factor. Tell her it's hers, and "borrow" it during season. She'll love it.

Once your excuse bag is full, you'll need to practice some of the finer points of grouse and woodcock hunting to make your day complete. One of these fine points is the art of falling down in a cover.

Now, sooner or later, you are going to take a dive. Most covers that I hunt are so thick that even if you fall, you'll never hit the ground. But for the purposes of enlightenment, we should know how to fall, and how to categorize these falls.

The first type of fall is what I call the "Cape Buffalo," or the "Stick Trick." In this one, the toe of one foot strikes a small limb or branch on the ground. In lifting that foot, the branch lifts, the opposite end embeds itself in the ground, and the foot cannot come down. Forward momentum takes over, and the laws of physics enter the picture in that a solid body with mass cannot be suspended at the horizontal for any length of time before gravity reaches up and grabs it.

When this happens, the stickee places his other foot down farther ahead of where it should have been, the next step is even longer, and soon we are getting to see the cover at a speed associated with a taxiing jetliner. Naturally, the end result is to go face first to the forest floor. To execute this one correctly, one must look for the proper object on which to land. Since much of my woodcock hunting is done near cattle pastures, I usually emerge from the cover at the speed of an untamed juggernaut and tour the pasture. I'll leave it to your imagination about where I usually end up coming down. Degree of difficulty: 1.7.

Another type of fall is the "Deadfall Dawdle." This one happens when the shooter decides to cross over a downed tree, brush pile, or what have you. Once atop the deadfall, be sure to stop to scan the horizon or look for your dog. The laws of biology governing decaying vegetation in the temperate zone will take over, guaranteeing that the key limb in the pile will give way at this point, and you'll plunge earthward like the trap door on a gallows has been opened. To have this fall count, you must be unable to emerge from the downfall for at least fifteen minutes. Degree of difficulty: 2.5.

A third type of fall commonly used is the "Mossy Rock Shuffle." This one is executed when crossing streams, rivers, or ditches in woodcock cover. Naturally, wishing to remain dry, we choose the path across that has the best series of rocks to use as, well, stepping stones. Pick out the kind covered with the algae known as *spirogyra*, as this is the most slippery. When one foot hits the slippery rock, it will fly out from under you and be replaced by the other foot. When this one also flips skyward, the first foot is back for a second turn. The end on this fall comes when both feet are pointed at the sky at the same time, and the splash in the closest, deepest pool takes place. Degree of difficulty: 2.5. Extra points for keeping the action going for longer than thirty seconds and for all trout scared to death by your entry into the water. Real pros get extra points for eye-bulging, mouth-gaping, and shotgun-losing.

The last type of tumble takes concentration and team-work. This is the "Pothole Plunge" and takes place under tightly-controlled conditions. The conditions are: The dog is on point, it is obviously your shot, the cover is open, and there is nothing to distract you from shooting and scoring. You advance slowly, the dog steadies. Just as you hear the bird flush, you step into a depression in the ground left by the roots of an overturned tree, long since decayed. You get the same feeling when you are walking down a flight of steps reading the paper, think there are no more steps, and there are. You disappear, the bird flushes, you can't even see it to shoot. Partner is convulsed with glee. Degree of difficulty: 3.0. Extra points if the dog had a double pinned, and they both flew straightaway.

If you can nail down the odd laugh or two from things that happen naturally, what about the contrived situation? In other words, what about the Practical Joke? Certainly, this piece of Americana can be used to spice up a day when the birds just can't be located, or when the weather is just too miserable to get serious about the whole thing. Practical jok-ing can take many forms, and my kid brother Eric, is perhaps the greatest PJ'er presently in captivity. What he hasn't done to punch up a hunting trip already, he'll come up with this season—he has a new bag of jokes every year, and I always tumble.

For example, I like a cup of coffee about midmorning and carry a thermos when I remember it. Two years ago last Christmas, Eric gave me a nice white coffee mug with my name on it and a picture of a flighting woodcock hand painted on the other side. I was thrilled. I should have saved my thrills. The next fall, I decided to initiate the cup on the drive up to the first cover on opening day. I was alone and whistling contentedly to myself. Steering the Jeep with my knee, I filled the new mug. As I savored the early-morning coffee, I suddenly felt hot and wet at the same time. Seems Kid Brother had drilled a small hole in the bottom of the cup and sealed it with paraffin wax. As the coffee heated the wax, it melted, and the coffee leaked out. There I was—55 miles an hour and a cup like the *Andrea Doria*. Plenty of fun—for Eric.

Another time, Eric gave me a half dozen handloaded 20-gauge shells he wanted me to try. He sort of casually dumped a handful of them into my shooting vest pocket and said no more about them. I should have smelled a rat.

Along about noon, he and I got into a good concentration of 'cock, and we both shot quite a few shells. I'd run out of skeet loads and then remembered the gift shells—the "special handloads." As the dog came on point, I groped for the shells Eric had given me. Tough luck. Seems he'd superglued the brass ends of the shells into one huge mass. He finished shooting that cover alone.

Just this past season, he pulled the ultimate PJ, the one from which I'm still trying to recover. For years, a small parcel of land that has a superb cover on it has been for sale by a downstate landowner. I'd always had permission to hunt this choice little corner, provided it never was sold. I happened to mention this to Eric once. Bad mistake. The rat ran out and bought signs which read "sold" and plastered them all over the cover. I stayed away from the cover, swearing at real estate agents in general, until his wife spilled the beans on him. I'd missed great shooting there all season. But did the cover go untouched? No. Eric hunted it when I wasn't around.

Machines

Machinery has a spirit. A mean, demonic, cursed little spirit placed here from hell to give me a bad time.

Right now, looking around me, I can see flashlights with perfect switches, bulbs, and batteries but they won't light; I see shooting glasses with screws that won't stay tight; I see knives that won't open and gun cases that won't close. The more advanced machines—things like can openers and cars and computers—baffle me. They were made to torment me.

I can hear them talking at night when they think I'm asleep. They discuss who will break next and when and where.

The thermos wants to get his cap cross-threaded the next time it's -12° in a goose pit.

The 4x scope says it will get fogged up on the inside the next time I crawl 600 yards on my belly after an antelope just at twilight.

And the bindings on the snowshoes plan to break when I'm four miles from the car, a half hour from dark, and in snow up to my crotch.

When I get up to check, they become very still.

But I know.

Bow Hunting Terminology
For Beginners

Not too long ago I was trapped in the company of known bow hunters, men who, save this one bit of organized lunacy, were in every way normal.

Now, the first thing I noticed right off was that none of these men appeared to be speaking the mother tongue of Americans. In fact, they used a language with which I was completely unfamiliar. This bothered me a bit until I discovered that they were using phrases and words associated with bow hunting. This really bothered me because I didn't know WHAT the hell they were talking about.

As a grouse and woodcock hunter, I am unfamiliar with the situation of being totally ignorant on any topic. Partially ignorant on all topics, maybe, but that's different. Those of us who hunt behind blooded setters and shoot dainty side-bysides are respected in outdoor circles as patrons of the arts, knowledgeable in the ballet, the opera, and fine literature. To admit ignorance of this "bow hunting" subject would have lowered the prestige which we, as a class, enjoy.

So, I simply kept my mouth shut and listened, in itself a feat, and I was able to discern some meanings of terms these bow hunters readily bandied about. But not content with partial knowledge, I visited my neighbor, an admitted bow hunter.

Crazy Charlie, as he's regarded locally, and with good reason, was behind his garage attempting to execute a large bale of straw which he had posted against the back of that structure. I watched for a bit and noticed that the guy was pretty good. He hit the garage about three shots out of five, and a couple times while I was there, he hit the bale with one of his little sticks with feathers on it. On one occasion, he even impaled the picture of a deer that he had stuck to the straw, much to his obvious delight. I was properly impressed and started my interrogation, again, feigning some knowledge of his sport.

From what Crazy Charlie told me, his shooting accuracy was commensurate with the average bow hunter's skill. I accepted this as fact because Charlie, above all else, is average.

Next, I quizzed him about the terms I'd heard the other bow hunters tossing around. I couldn't press the issue of asking for too much detail without giving the impression that I was not well versed on the subject because this would have, naturally, damaged my well-deserved reputation as the Neighborhood Answer Man.

Therefore, for the benefit of others who find themselves with little substantive knowledge of bow hunting jargon, I have set forth the following dictionary of terms. These are here bequeathed in the way that I learned them, and in no particular order, which seems appropriate.

Shaft—I'm pretty sure that this refers to the little sticks that the bow hunter shoots at his target or game. Sometimes called arrows, the term "shaft" comes from the price of these sticks as they are bought by the dozen—as in, "Boy, I sure got the shaft!"

Recurve—This no doubt refers to a spinal condition which comes from two related activities: trying to pull back the bowstring and falling out of a tree stand.

Compound Bow—A bow with little wheels all over it that is supposed to make the shooter more proficient. The name comes from the type of interest on the loan necessary to buy such an instrument.

Tree Stand—A platform in a tree from which bow hunters regularly do the following: miss deer with all their little sticks; miss feeding grouse with all their little sticks; miss rabbits with all their little sticks; execute half-gainers from the pike position trying to clamber down to retrieve their little sticks at sunset. It should be noted that after a shot is taken at a deer, the average bow hunter quickly engages in a closely related game entitled "Find the Arrow."

Knock Knock

"Who's there?"

"Betcha"

"Betcha who?"

"Betcha can't climb a tree stand, get a deer, and find all your arrows during the same lifetime."

Quiver—What a prospective bow hunter does when informed of the price of the equipment. Also, what every bow hunter does when his wife finds the receipts. Closely related to buck fever, but the bucks in this case are much bigger and carry pictures of former presidents.

Broadhead—Similar to "recurve" in that it probably describes a cranial condition having to do with the abrupt halt of the human body after it has left a tree stand, attained escape velocity, and met Mother Earth.

Fred Bear—Apparently the patron god of archers and bow hunters. Some particularly devout cultists have little plaster statues of this deity in their backyards.

The Rut—A time of the fall bow hunting season when the

hunting is evidently the best because the physical condition of swollen necks, slavering tongues, and apparent disregard for physical safety make getting a deer easier. Since all bow hunters at one time or another exhibit these bodily phenomena, I can't see how it helps them.

The Parson And
The Crabapple Dog

The Parson had never seen the dog before. He walked out of the little country church that had been his life— along with Mabel—for thirty-seven years, and there sat the dog.

It wasn't much of a dog, really, just sort of one part that was setter and one part that wasn't. The Parson probably wouldn't have noticed him but he'd looked down as he walked by the crabapple tree and there sat the dog, shaded from the afternoon sun. The Parson spent a lot of time these days walking around with his head down and his eyes averted from those who might pass him by. He guessed he didn't want anybody to look into his eyes, the "windows to the soul," as the Greeks used to say.

If anyone had looked into his eyes, they would have seen

that the Parson was a mighty sad man. Mabel's death in the spring had left him alone and hurting. More than that, it had left him bitter. The Parson had never known bitterness before, and the taste wasn't sweet at all. He guessed that's why it was called what it was.

Life had been sweet when he'd had Mabel. True, there hadn't been any children, and this always bothered him because he knew it had bothered her, but the church and the needs of the congregation these many years had always been enough. Since she had gone away in the spring, he'd been having some very unparsonlike thoughts.

He knew the feelings by rote, having seen them second-hand among the families of his flock whom he'd counseled after a loved one had died. The shock, the anger, the feeling that God had forsaken them, and finally the grief and acceptance and the return of faith.

But for the Parson, the time had long passed when his own emotions should have been centered on grief and acceptance. He had locked in on the helpless rage, a rage at an uncaring God who would take his partner from him, a partner who had done so much good for God. Weeks had passed since her death, but the feeling didn't pass. This was why he had his head down that late summer day and this is how he saw the dog sitting in the shade of the fruit-laden crabapple tree in the churchyard. Funny, the blossoms were just coming out the day he'd buried Mabel.

As he trudged toward the parsonage, the dog fell in step next to him. Following him home, the dog only made one sound, a pitiful whine as the screen door closed behind the clergyman. At the sound, the Parson turned, hesitated for a moment, and opened the door. The dog marched in as if it were his due and dropped to the kitchen floor with a bony flop.

After a simple meal, for he had little appetite, the Parson thought about the dog for a moment and offered him the remains of his dinner. The dog hungrily devoured it and again took his sitting position. The Parson headed for the door to take his evening walk, and the dog followed, as before, in step with the man. They headed for the creek that ran through the woods behind the house.

The late evening sun was setting as they crossed the bridge over the creek, now at low-water stage. The dog bounded off the end of the bridge into the thick alders that grew along the bank and rustled around in the brush. Mildly curious, the Parson stopped, leaned against the rail of the bridge and watched. After a time, the rustling stopped and there was no sound. Fearing the dog might be injured, the clergyman stood erect, then followed the last sound he'd heard into the alders and thick grasses.

He found the dog quickly. The large white patches made him easy to see even in the fading light. He noticed that the dog was pointing, his semi-setter tail high and not flagging. Walking forward, the Parson almost stepped on a woodcock as it twittered up between the branches of the alders. The Parson was surprised, the dog was nonchalant. Three more times before the light failed, the dog found and pointed woodcock and the Parson flushed them.

They walked home together in the sunset's afterglow, the dog in his now-accustomed spot, the Parson feeling better than he had in weeks. The outdoors had always made him feel good, and with the excitement he'd experienced with his new-found friend, the feeling was doubled.

At home, in the parsonage again, the man rummaged around in the attic for his old shotgun. As a student, he had loved to hunt, especially upland birds—pheasants mostly— but he had read some books on woodcock and grouse hunting. Finding his gun, his father's old L. C. Smith 16-gauge, he set about cleaning it up. The shooting season was several weeks off—opening in mid-September—but he thought he might see if the old gun would take service. It might be good to get away a day or two this season. He always was able to think better in the woods anyway.

The season came, and, when it did, he and his dog— dubbed "Crab"—knew most of the woodcock by their first names. The opening morning, the dog pointed six birds and the Parson shot two. They had been easy chances, but inexperience with woodcock made him slow. Several days later, they got out again, and this time the Parson shot three woodcock and missed a grouse. The following Monday, he shot his first grouse, and that night's dinner was in the bag.

As the season progressed, the Parson found himself looking forward to each day. The colors had never been this vivid before, he thought. He started to feel that he and the dog had a good bond, a solid one, like he and Mabel once had — still had.

The Parson took to wearing his gunning clothes under his cleric's robes on Sundays. After services, he would warmly greet each worshipper and then scamper off to the woods behind the house for a hunt. The people around town even started to comment that the Parson was his old self again, like before Mabel died. The Parson heard their talk and thought of Mabel. The bitterness was still there, but the fire that had raged within him was starting to smolder.

One day in early November, the woodcock started to flight. He and Crab were out that day. The Parson shot his limit of five birds with five right barrels from the now-true Smith. The day was rare for November, warm and with a touch of September — no, April — in the air. He couldn't remember a late autumn day like it.

He and Crab sat down beneath a big white oak, a tree that had been a sapling when the lumbermen had gone through and taken out the pine a century before. It had been a short hunt, but the Parson was tired. He leaned back against the tree and dozed in the sun-dappled leaves.

As he dozed, he thought of Mabel. He hadn't thought of Mabel for quite a few days, now. He hated the bitterness toward . . . well, toward the POWERS THAT BE for taking her from him, so he had thought of Crab and his shooting instead. But, this day, he thought of Mabel. He thought of how she would have liked Crab. He thought of how she would have loved the autumn woods. He thought of how she would have been ashamed of him for neglecting his congregation the way he had done, and finally, he thought of how she would have been shocked and dismayed to know of his inner bitterness toward the God he had sworn to serve—and had served—these many years.

With little warning except a sting in his nose, the tears came. He cried for Mabel. He cried for himself and he cried for the feelings he had harbored and nurtured these past months since she had died. As he cried, he felt changed— changed back, in the sense he was more like he had been before Mabel left him—before Mabel had "gone home."

He opened his eyes, finally, to find the mist rising from the stream not far away. He could hear the water gurgling along, thanks to the rains that had come in October, and thought it was good. He thought the world was a little better than when he had sat down. In fact, it was better than it had been for months—since last spring.

He knew that Crab had been a part of it. Crab and the grouse and the woodcock and the coverts had been a tonic for him. He had taken a liberal dose and found it had worked—it had just taken time.

He cast his eyes around toward the sound of shuffling leaves. Crab was up and ambling away. The dog stopped about twenty yards from him and turned to look at the man over his shoulder. The look told the man not to follow, not to call. It was a strangely familiar look.

With that, the dog turned and was gone. The man sat for long moments sorting out what had happened. Finally, he stood and picked up the old L.C. Smith. He broke the gun and cradled it in his right arm.

He turned, and with quick steps, headed toward the parsonage. He had work to do. A congregation to look after. And it was high time he was getting to it. Yessir.

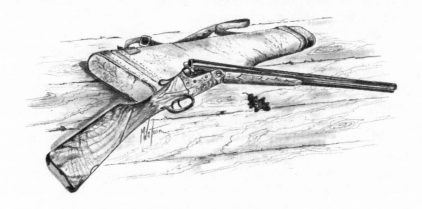

The Markers To Time

An old shotgun is a piece of the past, a past we were not around for, and probably wouldn't have appreciated if we had been.

I've got a 16-bore Parker, not a very high grade, but it still cost me quite a few times more than it cost the original owner when he had it built in 1927.

What I like about this Parker I'm keeping is that it must have belonged to a true bird hunter because this gun is a real sixteen—straight stock, splinter forearm, and a couple ounces under six pounds. It's bored open improved cylinder and improved modified with two triggers.

What I like about it is that it's a slice of time, it takes me away to past days and past seasons. When I carry it down a wooded path toward the car after an October hunt, I always look around to see if anyone's watching. If they are, I sort of hope they've read *New England Grouse Shooting* and recognize me and my sweetfooted little orange Belton setter for what we think we are, throwbacks to a past era, when the sixteen was an experienced wingshot's gun—the "gentleman's gauge."

Matter of fact, there are a lot of dinosaurs out there, hunters who cherish what the game department people like to call the "quality experience." Normally, that means you won't see many birds—I think it means appreciating a day in the coverts for what it is, a bit of timelessness.

I wonder about the other Parker owners, and those who carry L.C. Smiths, A.H. Foxes, or those who gun their birds with real Ithacas. I should call them "keepers," because they're only guiding the guns through the present from their past.

I wonder about my friends who cringe at sleet and steel shot and then gird their collective loins and hike into a duck blind with these old classics because the wind and the sky and the call—and the kill—are so timeless that the gun should be, too.

It seems a little strange to waste this type of emotion on an unfeeling chunk of walnut and steel, and I don't suppose most people would understand. No matter. We're not talking to them. We're talking to those who value a leg-o-mutton gun case and a real, living, 16 bore over a factory-stamped, photo-engraved, machine-checkered marvel picked up at a discount store. Nothing wrong with these, I suppose, except that the odd time or two when I've gunned with one, I've felt a little factory-stamped and machine-checkered. I gun the wood-cock flights with my 16 because it seems right. Pretty simple, really.

My waterfowl gun is what some call the Perfect Repeater, a Model 12 Winchester in 12 bore, bought by my dad the day I was born for what would be a morning's wages today for most of us. Now Dad really threw his money around, back then. Well, I've got his gun. Actually, I'm keeping it until my own son gets long enough in the arms to handle the stock. Meanwhile, I'll take good care of it.

Slogging through the predawn mud toward a duck blind, I wonder what it must have felt like to be carrying a Model 12 toward some trench in France along about 1918 or so, the magazine crammed with 00 buck and my throat crammed with heart.

Then, I imagine I'm on the Susquehanna Flats ready to start my day of shooting for the market, and my partner is my pickup man, the dog a Chessie with the heart of a lion and faithful to me alone.

Labor day a few years back, and I was up early, but not as early as Gene Hill three states away. The phone rang and this familiar voice on the other end told me, "When Hill's up, everybody's up!" We chatted a minute about some business, and he told me he was going dove hunting that day across the river in Pennsylvania and mentioned he was going to take his fine old Hussey hammer gun 12 bore. I remarked that I would have to look around for a hammer gun because I didn't have one. He offhandedly asked me if a 16 would interest me, knowing my affection for that gauge and I told him sure and that he should keep his eyes open.

Two weeks later, the gun arrived—a 16 gauge hammer gun. My gunsmith called to say it was in and that Hill had called him for the proper shipping permits but told him to stay quiet about it. There's a note on it. The note is private. This gun is special because of its own heritage—coming from the collection of a man as special to me as Hilly. I can't look at it without seeing him.

The dogs that hunt with us the few, precious seasons they have on earth jog us, too. We track them through their pedigrees and through the good talk about this strain or that line, and we recall points and retrieves, and skunks and porcupines and the graying muzzles that mark the passing of seasons.

More than anything, I think that's what I like about old guns and old dogs, and old friends. They're the markers of time.

October Third

The battle starts at dusk. The sun dies early, and night rushes on to count coup. The sky fights a losing struggle for life.

It is then that the woodcock come, refugees in flight against the twilight, pushed by the front. They are sprouted and spewed upward from the alders and the aspens like seedpods in a chapparal fire. If you stand with me, shivering outside the car parked on a hill, you can see them coming, too.

And in that last bit of candlepower before the earth swallows the sun, you can see them drop into the Home Coverts. The next day, my dogs and I will be there, greeting them as we have for decades. Woodcock are autumn.

The Home Coverts are close to me, in the neighborhood

of my home. It is to these places that I sneak off when work gets tedious. It is here I take some friends—those from out of state—and we enjoy a few days of grand shooting.

In the home coverts, I took a pal from Houston. He had never done much woodcock shooting; he came from a world of ducks and geese and quail and doves. But he had read the stories and seen the paintings, and he was ready. He shot woodcock, and he missed woodcock, and in the home coverts, he learned to love woodcock. He learned to love pointing dogs with floppy jowls, and he learned to love the occasional grouse that got his nervous system cleaned out, and he learned to love my part of the world.

He no longer lives in Houston. He lives in a part of the world where the crashing-surf clouds scudding before a front push the woodcock along. He lives where the color changes like a thing alive, and he now has his own home coverts. He doesn't make as much money now, and he has setter hair on all the good furniture and in his favorite Scotch glass. But he doesn't care. The woodcock have taken the caring from him. They come on the wind and they leave in the night, and for a few days offer the grandest sport at the grandest time of year. He loves it here, and here he is welcome.

Woodcock do that to a man—and so does autumn.

Pick a day—any day. Make it your favorite of the year. I don't mean Christmas or the day your mother-in-law leaves for Wrinkle City, Florida, I mean a genuine autumn day when things are just right.

My day is October third. It is then that many, many good things have happened to me. October third has been on my side for some time, now, and I expect it will continue.

For one thing, the woodcock are coming, and the home coverts have dropped enough leaves to make actually shooting a bird a bit more likely than, say, winning a lottery or having your kid get all As on his finals.

For another thing, the ducks are there, waiting, and so are the geese and the pheasants. Later, there will be the trips to other places for different birds—Kansas for quail, and

Texas for snow geese, and Manitoba for sharptails. But right now, on my day, it is a time for staying home and being there.

October third sums up what we live for, you and me, the life that told us long ago to let others climb the corporate ladders and take the three-martini lunches. Ours is a world of dog hair on our only good suit, one pair of dress shoes and four pair of waders, lawns that need cutting, and storm windows that need washing. Our world—yours and mine—is filled with our autumn obsessions, and one is looking for that perfect season or even that one perfect day. For me, October third is that day in that most perfect of seasons.

I don't do much on that day. I have friends to see, and work can't get in the way. I have grouse to visit and geese to watch flying over, and maybe a buck to listen to as he snorts like an old man with bad adenoids. On this day, things seem at their best. There have been times when I was at my best, too, and it seems it was always on this day.

What I'm saying is that there will be other times in autumn for that grand shot, that perfect point, or that spread of blocks that could fool a stuffed mallard. October third is for enjoying and watching and feeling alive.

We live such a short time, and so much of it is taken up in achieving something or other—an education, a career, a family, a limit—that we don't take the time to take a day to do nothing except skylark and dream . . . and remember.

I hope your Octobers are fine and many. I hope your October thirds are as good to you as mine have been to me.

So as I end this book, it's only fitting that I tell you that tomorrow is October third, and I've got my plans made. Those plans center around enjoying life—after that, things get vague.